THE SEA PEOPLES AND EGYPT

THE SEA PEOPLES AND EGYPT

by
ALESSANDRA NIBBI

NOYES   PRESS

Park Ridge, New Jersey

Published in the United States by
NOYES PRESS
Noyes Building
Park Ridge, New Jersey 07656

Library of Congress Cataloging in Publication Data

Nibbi, Alessandra.
    The Sea Peoples and Egypt.

    Bibliography: p.
    Includes index.
    1. Sea Peoples. 2. Egypt—History—To 332 B.C.
I. Title.
DE73.2.S4N494   932'.01   75-33594
ISBN 0-8155-5041-3

CONTENTS

INDEX OF PLATES

ACKNOWLEDGEMENTS

Plates II, III, XII, XIII and all those in line drawings (Frontis-
piece, Plates I, VIII, IX, X, XI, XIV, XV, and XVI) are from Medinet
Habu and are reproduced by courtesy of the Oriental Institute,
University of Chicago.

Plates IV and VII are reproduced by courtesy of the Trustees of
the British Museum.

Plates V and VI: photographs, Ashmolean Museum, Oxford.

INDEX OF FIGURES

Frontispiece

From the Mortuary Temple of Ramesses III, Medinet Habu, kneeling bound captives from southern and northern countries; a limestone relief, somewhat damaged.

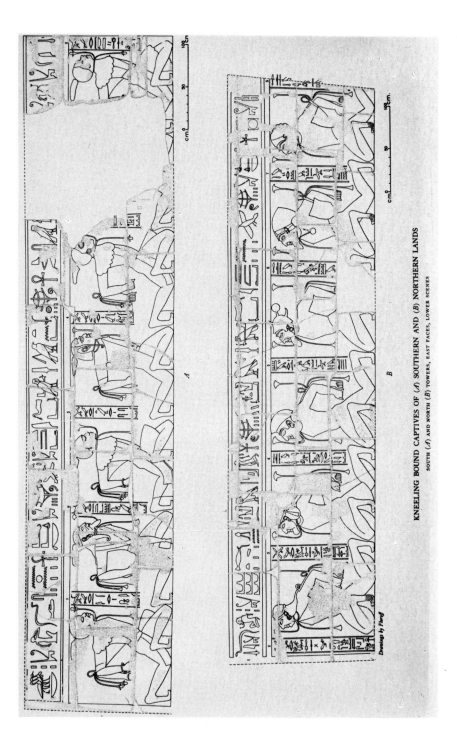

KNEELING BOUND CAPTIVES OF (A) SOUTHERN AND (B) NORTHERN LANDS

SOUTH (A) AND NORTH (B) TOWERS, EAST FACES, LOWER SCENES

Drawing by Faraj

PREFACE

When my short monograph appeared at the end of 1972 entitled *The Sea Peoples: A Re-examination of the Egyptian Sources*, a great deal remained to be said about some fundamental and closely related problems. The monograph had been produced in haste in time to be circulated before the Third International Colloquium on Aegean Prehistory, held in Sheffield in 1973, on the same subject. My intention was to draw attention to the content of the texts relating to the Sea Peoples, which have been almost totally ignored until now.

Besides revealing that the so-called Sea Peoples were Egypt's traditional Asiatic enemies, the examination of these texts has produced some further surprising results which are discussed in this volume:

> (a) that "Great Green" never means 'sea' in the Egyptian texts and that ym means 'sea' only sometimes; this affects many basic concepts concerning Egypt's geographical limits;
>
> (b) that a large part of the Delta was completely foreign territory for the Egyptians until very late times, the Retenu (or Kharu) beginning *inside* the Delta, in the eastern, Asiatic-occupied sector;
>
> (c) that Egypt was an inland country, cut off from the sea until very late times, all the evidence suggesting that they never went to sea but relied on Asiatic shipping and crews.

Basically what I am saying is quite simple. We should take the texts literally and accept what they say at face value as far as we can. The consequences of this, however, are very complex and far-reaching. I do not pretend that I have done them full justice here. All I can hope to do is to throw a fresh light on these problems to stimulate further discussion on them.

My thanks are due to many people who have helped me, without necessarily sharing my views: the late professors J. Černý and J. W. B. Barns and also Dr. J. Málek, all of whom were always ready to assist me with language and bibliography, Mr. W. V. Davies who discussed many points with me, Miss Helen Murray through whose kind offices the archives of the Griffith Institute were available to me, and Mrs. Joan Crowfoot Payne and Dr. R. Moorey, the specialists with regard to the Egyptian collection at the Ashmolean Museum.

It has been a privilege and a pleasure to work in the Griffith Institute and the Ashmolean Library, with such knowledgeable and helpful librarians and staff. To Mrs. Pat Clarke my special thanks are due for many of the drawings in this volume.

My gratitude to the British Museum should also be recorded, particularly to Dr. I. E. S. Edwards, Dr. T. G. J. James and Mr. A. F. Shore, whose patient answers to my early questions enabled me to take my first tentative steps in this subject.

Alessandra Nibbi
Oxford, 1975

Alessandra Nibbi is a graduate of Florence University. Her early years were spent in Australia where her father, Gino Nibbi, was an art critic, journalist and writer. She attended the University of Melbourne and also taught for a time at the University of Sydney, before returning to Italy.

It was in Florence that Dr. Nibbi was first able to indulge fully her interest in the ancient history of the Mediterranean. As a result of her consideration of the Etruscans, she began research in Egyptology at Oxford, in order to pursue the Turush to their original sources. She has continued working in this field ever since, and now lives in Oxford.

The Problem of the Sea Peoples

There has been growing pressure on scholars of Aegean, Anatolian and Near Eastern archaeology in recent years to make more sense of the phenomena occurring at the end of the Bronze Age, namely the destruction which occurred in widespread areas and the subsequent changes in the material culture of the new settlements. This has always been explained as a migration of peoples of which the Sea Peoples were considered to be the main stream. Yet since this theory appeared with the first reading of the Egyptian texts of the Ramesside period, just over one hundred years ago, these Sea Peoples have remained shrouded in mystery and no one has been able to say more of them than that they came from the north and that their names sounded like those of people we know from later times.

Scholars today see this question in terms of two major attacks on Egypt approximately fifty years apart by great numbers of people from an unknown north finding their way southwards and wanting to settle in Egypt. We may sum up the general view of the problem in the words of Hans Goedicke:

> The character of these thrusts has never been properly considered. Sometimes called a migratory movement of great dimension, such an identification is inappropriate by the Egyptian records. . . . The undeniable problems of a confederation between Libyans and an array of foreigners with different backgrounds remains as unanswerable as the purpose of this federation and the aim and logistics of their attack.[1]

1

In his chapter on "The Sea Peoples" for the *Cambridge Ancient History*, Dr. R. D. Barnett spoke of the "bewildering tangle of evidence, much of it highly fragmentary" relating to this problem.[2] He was right. Nothing except the Egyptian texts of this period really tells us anything about the attackers of Egypt. This is a remarkable fact which ought to have given us a clue before now. Probably what has misled us is the perennially troubled history of the Near Eastern city states, which seemed to be continually making and breaking alliances among themselves, quite apart from their relationship with Egypt.

Yet the destruction too was of a fragmentary nature, some cities being destroyed and others not, suggesting factions rather than totally hostile hordes. We must not hope to find in the Sea Peoples the answer to all the destruction of cities at the end of the Bronze Age. One is encouraged by the more objective methods now being used by archaeologists in these areas and by their conclusions which do not require an invasion of peoples from the north.

There is only one scientific method of investigation and that is to examine the evidence. Almost all the evidence we have for the Sea Peoples is in the Egyptian texts. The few fragments and clues found elsewhere and discussed in our chapter on pictorial evidence, are never in a related context which we can understand. So it is to the texts that we must turn. We must examine their contents as carefully as we can and draw only the conclusions to which they lead us. These are very different from the traditional picture of the Sea Peoples presented by the textbooks.

It must be admitted that Egyptologists are innocently responsible for the false picture of this problem which has arisen. These texts were immediately available to the early Egyptologists because they were written on visible stone monuments, though sometimes difficult of access. With a tremendous wave of enthusiasm, they were read, interpreted and then set aside. Egyptologists have been busy with problems of language and grammar since then. Much work has been done in publishing documents and inscriptions during all these years. It is only now that we may expect fresh attention to be drawn to them as a result of this freshly aroused controversy. This will vindicate those few fine scholars who have spent much time and labour on these texts, the Medinet Habu team from the Oriental Institute of

Chicago[3] and particularly W. F. Edgerton and J. A. Wilson, whose *Historical Records of Ramesses III* has brought us much closer to the texts than we could ever otherwise have come today.[4]

What must be stressed is that the question of the Sea Peoples was misplaced from the very first readings of the texts owing to a complexity of errors which arose together. The history of these errors is outlined elsewhere[5] and will not be repeated here. However, attention must be drawn to the basic misconceptions themselves which have caused all the trouble.

The naming of these attackers of Egypt as the "Sea Peoples" seems to have been cemented by an article in 1881 by Gaston Maspéro in which he called them "peuples de la mer,"[6] an expression which caught everyone's imagination and has remained fixed, we fear, forever. He had good reason for using this expression. Some of the texts (to which we shall refer in detail later) did speak of some of these peoples as being "of the ym." This is true of the Ekwesh in the Karnak and Athribis texts from the time of Merenptah; the Sherden and the Turush of the ym are mentioned at Medinet Habu, while the Papyrus Harris refers to the Sherden and the Weshesh in this way. Ym is a Semitic word which came to be used in the Egyptian language after the Hyksos presence in Egypt, that is, from the eighteenth dynasty onwards. The expression 'great ym' is used in the story of Wenamun for Mediterranean, but that use is quite unusual, and in that case is qualified further by calling it "the great ym of Kharu." Its normal use is for any stretch of inland water and we believe that it is this meaning that applies in these texts, the ym referring to the water of the Nile after it had dispersed into the marshes of the Delta and into the area of the Bitter Lakes. These are the regions to which we believe these Egyptian texts refer.

However, there were further complications. As early as 1836, J. F. Champollion had recognised the Peleset as Philistines,[7] a reasonable assumption which no one has questioned until today. The scholars of his day strove to identify the other attackers of Egypt by the similarity of their names to peoples known in antiquity. Hence the Sherden from Sardinia, the Shekelesh from the Siculi in Sicily, the Lukka from Lycia and so on. The only reason for any of these parallels is the similarity of the sounds of these names. Such reasoning must be set aside. Nevertheless, we have continued to assume that the Peleset were Philistines on the slender evidence of the clay anthropoid sarcophagi found in Palestine, carrying markings showing exactly the same head-dresses with the varying bands of ornamentation that we find in the Egyptian reliefs.[8]

It is with these identifications that the trouble began. The argument was that, if Egypt's attackers included the Sardinians and Sicilians, they had to come to Egypt by sea, so ym was interpreted as 'sea'. The Sherden having thus been given a homeland, the "Sherden of the Great Green" required "Great Green" to mean 'sea' also. It is as a consequence of these texts that the expression "Great Green" came to be interpreted as 'sea' by Egyptologists, even though we cannot find a single case where this translation is justified from the context.

It followed that "the middle islands of the Great Green" and any other island which the early Egyptologists found were placed in the Mediterranean or in the Red Sea. Yet again, even today we have no evidence of any reference to an island outside the Nile until the time of Wenamun. The only way in which people will find a reference to Crete or Cyprus in the earlier texts is by forcibly interpreting them in this way.[9]

The fact that these attackers of Egypt were called "northern hill-countries" seemed to carry no weight in this early period of Egyptological studies. We know today that this expression refers only to the western Asiatic city states and to no others. For Egypt, the North began with the Delta, which was called the North Land. We have devoted a special chapter to this topic which we believe is fundamental to a proper interpretation of any texts relating to western Asia and also to Egypt's fundamental geography. We believe this area has been insufficiently understood until now, although it is encouraging to see that Dr. J. Yoyotte is joining with a few others in opening up the study of the topography and also the toponymy of these areas.[10]

The so-called Sea Peoples were said to have made "a conspiracy in their isles." This reference to the hostile groups as "islands" must be taken literally. We believe all the Egyptian texts must be taken literally. We say in our chapter on the Delta that it was extensively settled with Asiatics who would have had to live on elevated areas of land, hence 'islands', made necessary by the swampy nature of the terrain there. We would also draw attention to the fact that every Asiatic fortress or *migdol* was built on an island, because it was surrounded by water. Every

Egyptian representation of an Asiatic town or fortress includes this detail. The Ramesside relief showing the town of Tunip clearly represents its base similarly to an 'island' sign (PlateXII).[11]

It has always been a matter of some surprise to scholars that Egypt's attackers were allied to the Libyans and fought together with them both in the Libyan cause and in their own. However, taking into account the reality of the foreign nature of the Delta to Egypt, and its traditional hostility recorded in the list of Nine Bows by its appearance as t3 mḥw , this common cause with Libya is no longer surprising. The future study of Lower Egypt and the Delta, and particularly the eastern Delta, will be most exciting and rewarding. Already the work of the Austrian excavations at Tell ed-Dabʿa, under the capable direction of Dr. M. Bietak, is promising great rewards.[12] It is to be hoped that the following chapters will provoke and stimulate further interest and discussion of these problems.

A further point which must be made about the so-called Sea Peoples is that some of them were circumcised, a fact which was recognised, respected and recorded by the Egyptian officials. The records from the reign of Merenptah state clearly in the lists of captives and slain that the allies of the Libyans were circumcised while the Libyans were not. This determined whether their phalli or their hands were subsequently cut off as trophies of war.[13]

We are resolutely refraining in this study from adding any more speculation or discussion about the *names* of these peoples as they appear in the records, beyond a very brief speculative note in our concluding paragraphs. We believe that no good purpose can be served by adding to the volume of such writing. We also feel that there is very little that we can accurately say about it at present. On this subject there will have to be a joint effort by various disciplines if any valid progress is to be made.

Finally we must again refer to the texts. It is an unfortunate fact that throughout these discussions on the Sea Peoples only brief passages from the texts have been taken into consideration and quoted repeatedly. These passages have not been related to the whole text from which they were taken, nor to the total literature of the period. This has inevitably led to a misunderstanding of the brief passages themselves as well as of the general context in which they were set. It will take time to recover from these errors.

NOTES ON CHAPTER ONE

1. H. Goedicke, *JARCE* 8 (1969-1970): 323f.

2. R.D. Barnett, "The Sea Peoples," *CAH*, vol. II, chapter XXVIII (1969).

3. Oriental Institute, University of Chicago, *Medinet Habu*, 1930-1970.

4. W.F. Edgerton and J.A. Wilson, *Historical Records of Ramesses III* (Chicago, 1936).

5. A. Nibbi, *The Sea Peoples: A Re-Examination of the Egyptian Sources* (Oxford, 1972), chapter I.

6. G. Maspéro, *ZÄS* , 1881, p. 118.

7. J.F. Champollion, *Grammaire égyptienne* (1936), p. 180.

8. Y. Yadin, *The Art of Warfare in Biblical Lands* (London, 1963), pp. 344f.

9. A. Nibbi, "Further Remarks on w3d-wr, Sea Peoples and Keftiu," *Göttinger Miszellen*, 10 (1974).

10. S. Adams, "Recent Discoveries in the Eastern Delta," *Ann. Serv.* 55 (1958): 301ff.; J. Yoyotte, "Notes et documents pour servir à l'histoire de Tanis," *Kêmi*, XXI (1971): 35f.; also by Yoyotte, "Reflexions sur la topographie et la toponymie de la région du Caire," *Bull. de la Soc. Fr. d'Egyptologie*, 67 (1973).

11. A. Badawy, *Architecture in Ancient Egypt* (Massachusetts, 1966), fig. 30, opposite p. 172; A.W. Lawrence on ancient Egyptian fortifications in *JEA*, 51 (1965): 69ff.; also Gardiner, *JEA*, VI (1920): 107.

12. M. Bietak, *MDAIK*, 26 (1970).

13. A.H. Gardiner, *Ancient Egyptian Onomastica* (Oxford, 1947), vol. I, pp. 122* and 196*.

The Delta and Lower Egypt

One of the causes of confusion in assessing the important role played by the Asiatics of the Near Eastern areas in the history of Egypt has been that we have not properly understood Lower Egypt and the Delta, either in their physical or in their political structure. It has become a commonplace to say that the double crown of Egypt represents the union between Upper and Lower Egypt which took place at some time in the early dynasties, but we are still very far from understanding either the causes or the consequences of such a union, or even the precise geographical implications of the terms we are using.

However, it is becoming increasingly clear that Lower Egypt, and particularly the Delta, contained at all times a number of strong foreign elements which were often actively hostile to the Pharaoh. There was a long tradition of hostility in Lower Egypt to the Egyptian ruler, a hostility which was shared by some other areas as well, including Upper Egypt. Lower Egypt, called the North Land (t3 mḥw) by the ancient Egyptians, is to be found on the list of the Nine Bows, Egypt's traditional enemies, for as long as such a list existed.[1] We cannot agree with scholars who have said that the early references to the Nine Bows were not expressions of hostility. Of course we do not have any textual evidence for hostility in the pre-dynastic and early dynastic periods, but there is a great deal of pictorial material, together with objects of war, recording Egypt's troubles with her neighbours, Asiatics and others.

The Nine Bows are first mentioned in the Pyramid Texts, and are represented pictorially in the ancient texts by depicting nine bows together, or by the use of one bow accompanied by nine strokes. Among the earliest pictorial examples we have of the Bows are two from Hierakonpolis, on a vase and on the "Scorpion" mace-head[2] and another from the base of the statue of Djoser.[3] However, we do not find them listed by name until the reign of Amenophis III, as Professor Jean Vercoutter has shown in his admirable study.[4] Here it is made clear that although this list may often vary in content by the addition of the names of other hostile groups, the order of the list of Nine Bows remains surprisingly constant. We must emphasize too that Lower Egypt (or the North Land) is hardly ever omitted from the list of any period.

The study by Dr. E. Uphill in 1966 on the Nine Bows is a valuable contribution to this discussion in that he re-examines the work done until that date and then suggests a geographical setting for these peoples. His study followed upon the previous fundamental and painstakingly detailed work of Vercoutter, which, being so carefully based on the textual material, will never be superseded.

Vercoutter pointed out that we may have lists comprising only the Nine Bows, but also lists of the many different peoples adjoining Egypt, preceded by an enumeration of the Nine Bows, as for example, in a list from the north external wall of the hypostyle hall at Karnak.[5] Here an inscription dating from the time of Ramesses II carries a list showing t3 šm'w (Upper Egypt) followed by twelve Nubian names, then t3 mḥw (Lower Egypt) with a town determinative, followed by ḥ3w nbwt and six other Nine Bows, with fifteen Asiatic names behind them.[6] We should not assume that this order was accidental.

Many scholars have suggested that the Egyptian topographical lists are conventional and copied from previous lists. There is no doubt some truth in this observation. But what J. Simons said of the topographical lists relating to Western Asia could also apply to the lists of the Nine Bows: "Even those lists, which clearly stand in some genealogical relation to one or more of their predecessors, always prove on close and detailed examination to contain some material of their own."[7] Both types of lists are not as stereotyped, and therefore not as unreliable as has often been suggested.

   The documents from the time of Ramesses III often refer to the
Nine Bows in conjunction with the attackers of Egypt's frontier,
the so-called Sea Peoples, and in the one detailed list of the time,
Lower Egypt is included.[8] The enemies of that time are said to
be: "The ḥ3w nbwt, Naharin, Tunip, Tenep(?), Lower Egypt,
Pebekh, Katna, Isi, Menesen, the people of the western oases,
the people of the eastern desert, the Tehenu, Segerekh, Yer-
teg(?)" (see Plate I).[9] This represents one of the few cases where
the names of the Nine Bows are not in their traditional order, as
Professor Vercoutter has pointed out.[10] There is nothing conventional about this list from the Mortuary Temple at Medinet Habu,
and it does not seem as though Lower Egypt is there by the law of
inertia, because we cannot find a parallel for this list. There is no
reason to suppose that the names of some of the Nine Bows here
are carelessly mixed with those of North Syria, as has sometimes
been asserted. After all, this list is not exactly like any other list
and the difference may well be a matter of precision rather than
negligence. The association of those names with each other
should be accepted and worked upon rather than rejected
because it does not fit our present view of the facts.
   We need to study the Delta more thoroughly in the light of its
being, in its earliest history at least, a kind of no man's land in
which the Asiatics were more at home than the Egyptians. We
need to bear in mind the fact that it was always listed among
Egypt's traditional enemies, and that the lists of the Nine Bows
show enough variations for them not to be taken as mere
reproductions of earlier lists. There is every reason to think that
Lower Egypt's recorded hostility to the Pharaoh, from Egypt's
earliest history onwards, was real.
   The range of Egypt's enemies, as far as the documents show,
was limited to its neighbours in adjoining territories overland, as
we hope to clarify in the following pages.
   It is first of all important to understand the physical remote-
ness of the Delta for the people living along the Nile. It has not
yet generally been realized that the Delta was never a permanent
and open two-way system of communication with the outside
world, or even with the Mediterranean coast, until well into
Graeco-Roman times.
   Even as late as the time of Ramesses III, Lower Egypt was a
distant land, associated in the mind of the average Egyptian with
Asiatics. We have a hieratic ostracon from Deir El Medineh

which the late Professor Černý dated to the reign of Ramesses III, in which the Egyptian draughtsman Menna reveals his attitude to the foreign and remote North Land through his remonstrances to his son Peroy. "You are (engaged) in the wanderings of the swallow and her young ones. You have reached Lower Egypt (the North Land) on a great journey. You mingled with ʿ3mu (Asiatics) having eaten bread (mixed) with your blood."[11]

Ancient Egypt was an inland country. Its northern boundary was *not* the Mediterranean but the point where the Nile lost its identity as a river, at about 160 kilometres south of that sea. The Delta in very early times not only was not Egypt, it wasn't anything at all except swampland.

A good map of the Nile Delta will show a great many promontories, large and small, projecting into the Mediterranean, each of which has been an outlet for a stream of the Nile water at some stage or other, but not all of them remained open to the sea at the same time, of course. This river has always been recognised as having been slow to flow to the sea. What really happened was that it flowed into the Delta, and there lost itself in marshland.

Professor J. Gwyn Griffiths has already discussed in lucid detail the references in Hecataeus and Herodotus to the Delta and the concept of its being literally "the gift of the Nile" since it is formed from the deposits of the river.[12] He suggests a more precise rendering of this idea would be "the gift of Haʿpy or the Nile in its inundation."[13]

H. E. Hurst emphasized that in early times the Nile had many branches instead of the main ones in use today and that there must have been cross channels as well as lakes left by the river cutting across bends before any embankments were built, so that much of the Delta was washed over by the flood each year, leaving behind a large amount of swamp.[14]

Strabo spoke of the continuous confusion of the boundaries caused by the Nile at the time of its increases, "since the Nile takes away and adds soil, and changes conformations of lands. . . ."[15] When the Nile rose, the whole country was under water, except for the settlements, which were situated on natural hills or artificial mounds, which, viewed from a distance, resembled islands.

Dr. Robert M. Adams carried out an admirable study of the Diyala basin[16] and he stressed that natural levees, built up of silt or sand deposited primarily by flood waters, are, in fact, the dominant land-forms of the flood plain in general. A companion feature to the levee is the low-lying basin or back-swamp.

> In the Mesopotamian context . . . swamps and salt marshes are formed which shrink or even disappear during the heat and low-water of the summer. Depending on local topographic conditions, surface water in such depressions may or may not find its way back into the channel of the parent water-course, but in any case only far downstream. While supporting and giving refuge to a rich fauna, and while providing excellent forage for large herds of sheep and goats during the spring, these depressions offer no inducement to permanent settlement and ordinarily are characterized by soils too badly leached for agriculture.[17]

The result of the meandering course of a stream is that it continuously, if not rapidly, changes its course as a result of the tendency of its waters to erode along the outside bank of a bend while deposition is going on along the inside bank.[18]

What is most important for us to note is that during times of inundation, artificial canals may join in the fate of the natural ones. Very high motivation and a great deal of organized labour would be necessary to keep any artificial canals open each year for the whole 160 kilometres or more of the distance to the sea.

A study of the Delta carried out by the Survey Department of Egypt as long ago as 1906 warned us that as far as physical geography is concerned, the Nile Delta as a delta teaches its lesson less clearly than many another, situated in regions less developed. It says also:

> In modern times, and especially in the last hundred years, so much has been done in the canalization of the Delta that it is difficult to distinguish with any certainty between river arms and artificial canals, especially as an existing waterway may include lengths of both in its course. Today both the Rosetta and Damietta arms are contained within artificial banks and flood waters are thus conducted to the sea so that the usual characteristic features of the deltaic conditions, swamps, lagoons, frequently shifting channels, etc. are becoming rare as even the hitherto waste lands are being reclaimed and brought under cultivation.[19]

In early times, therefore, the Delta was largely an area of marshland and generally unsuited to settlement or agriculture until a systematic and regular system of canals was set up and maintained. We have no knowledge of the period in which the ancient Egyptians began to do this in the Delta, although the title of "canal-digger" is one of the oldest we have, dating from the times of Djoser and Snefru.[20] We also know that the importance of this activity was considered to be so great that people could be conscripted to dig canals if necessary.[21]

Recently two plant biologists, Keith Thompson and John Gaudet, carried out some studies on papyrus and its role in tropical swamps. They show clearly that the existence of a papyrus swamp requires undrained and uncultivated land.[22] Papyrus cannot grow where there is flood control or land drainage. Either will cause the disappearance of the plant. These scientists found that papyrus swamps in Uganda occur inland in valleys well away from any conspicuous body of water, and that papyrus will not grow where there is fast flowing water or where the level of the water is susceptible to much change.[23] These conditions are very significant and they help us to see the situation in the ancient Delta. The papyrus swamps which we know to have existed in ancient times cannot have been situated in the areas where the Nile water flowed into the sea, or where the land was drained, or cultivated. Nor can there have been papyrus growing along the main stream of the Nile.

Another point to be made here is that the abundant pictorial and textual references to lush fishing areas in the ancient documents point to a very definite swamp environment. In a study of the interaction between environmental factors and aquatic and semi-aquatic plants, Thompson confirmed that more fish are to be found in swamp waters than in the main streams of a river,[24] as Herodotus had said long ago.[25]

The Egyptian records tell us quite a lot about Lower Egypt and the Delta, but this information has not yet been given sufficient attention as direct evidence of the conditions existing in the area.

Unsuitable though this marshland must have been for agriculture in early dynastic times, the records of this same period show that the western peripheral area of the Delta was subject to administration of a kind and that vineyards, orchards and the cultivation of flax were to be found there.[26] Herman Kees noted that at the height of the Old Kingdom the estates of the Delta were often represented as the sources for funerary endowments of Memphite notables,[27] no doubt a way of encouraging the reclamation of potentially fertile land. He also noted how dispersed landed property was, which is not surprising if we bear in mind the nature of the land. Divided up as it was into small estates, separated from each other by water, marsh and islands in wholly undeveloped districts, no manorial estates were developed in Lower Egypt such as existed in Upper Egypt from the fifth dynasty onwards.[28] This was also the reason for the wide expanse of the nomes of Lower Egypt, compared to the smaller ones of Upper Egypt which Kees described. Strabo spoke of the "ten nomes" of the Delta.[29] But the eastern Delta had special problems of its own:

> Dig a dyke against (half) of it (the North Land) and flood half of it as far as the Bitter Lakes. Behold, it is the very navelcord of foreigners. Its walls are warlike and its soldiers many . . . . The region of Djed-sut . . . many northerners water it as far as the Northland, tax-free in grain. . . . They have made a dyke as far as Herakleopolis . . . guard against encirclement by the retainers of an enemy. . . . When thy frontier is endangered towards the (southern) region it means that the (northern) bowmen will take on the girdle. Build structures in the Northland. . . . [30]

These statements from the Instruction for Meri-Ka-Re, dating, according to Dr. J. A. Wilson, to the transition period between the Old and the Middle Kingdoms, clearly state the general situation for us, even if the detail remains rather nebulous.

From the reign of Mentuhotep II in the eleventh dynasty we have a reference to an army of 3,000 sailors "of the nomes of the Northland" who accompanied the large lid of a sarcophagus from the Wadi Hammamat quarries downstream to its destination.[31] No doubt this reflects a period of peace in Lower Egypt, since they could be spared from their duties there.

The Pharaoh must therefore have kept the eastern Delta well policed during this period and such large numbers of troops suggest that it can have been no easy task. This area was always a very troublesome one for Egypt, in spite of some natural defences in the form of swamplands and the building of the Egyptian fortress of Sile on the main pass through this swampland. The earliest textual reference to Sile (t3rw) is to be found in the records of Tuthmosis III,[32] but we know that the area was called earlier "the Ways of Horus" and was always policed. We learn this from the story of Sinuhe, who on his return to Egypt had to stop there to receive permission to continue his journey back into his native country.

It is not unreasonable to suppose that all the area in the eastern Delta beyond the road and the pass leading northwards was in reality a foreign land for Egyptians until as late as the Ramesside period. Hermann Kees noted that the list of nomes in the shrine of Sesostris I at Karnak lacks nomes 18-20 of the eastern Delta and also the Sebennytus nome. He concluded that these nomes must have come into existence only after the expulsion of the Hyksos.[33] However, the fortified frontier nome 14, "Front-of-the-East" with its "Ways of Horus" leading northwards, is mentioned in the list of Sesostris I. The reliefs from the time of Sethos I clearly show the fortresses protecting the wells on the road along which all Egyptian traffic to the northern countries had to travel, as our records indicate. The reliefs also show the canal, which was probably navigable, although it appears to be over-full of crocodiles[34] (fig. ·1).

The Instruction for Meri-Ka-Re gives us considerable geographical detail about Lower Egypt, which the Pharaoh at that time had tried hard to settle with his own people, to counterbalance the presence of so many foreigners there:

> He who arose (as) lord in a city arose with his heart troubled because of the Northland, Het-shenu to Sebaqa, with its southern boundary up to the . . . Canal. I pacified the entire west, as far as the coast of the (Great Green). . . . (But) the east is rich in bowmen, and their work. . . . Behold, (the area) which they injured is (now) made into nomes and all large cities. . . . The dues of the Northland are in thy hand. Behold, the mooring-stake is driven in the region which I have made in the east, up to the limits of Hebenu and as far as the Ways-of-Horus, settled with citizens and filled with people, the picked men of the entire land, in order to oppose their arms thereby.[35]

There can be no doubt that this is a deliberate policy of settlement in an area where the Egyptians clearly had been in a minority. Yet it seems that at this time, which appears to be the First Intermediate Period, the Egyptians had had to fight and establish their rights in the area which took them as far as the Ways-of-Horus and no further. They are now demanding taxes from this region, having established their sovereignty there. The text clearly emphasizes that such rights had to be upheld by the force of arms.

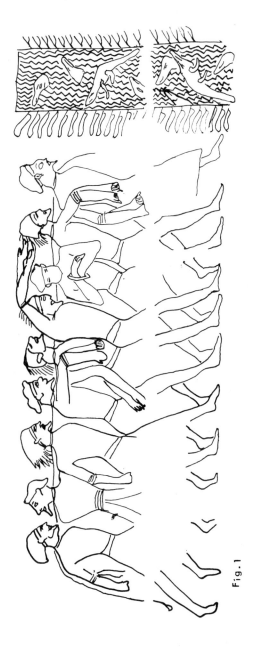

Fig. 1

Figure 1. A row of prisoners from the campaign against the Shosu-Beduin; from the reign of Sethos I.

We now have archaeological proof of Asiatic settlement of the Middle Bronze period in the eastern Delta at Tell ed-Dab'a, which antedates the Hyksos presence there.[36] There are many other reasons also for thinking that large numbers of Asiatics dwelt in the Delta from very early times, although they may not have been always hostile.[37]

The late Professor Černý noted that most of the inscriptions from the Sinai area are about hostilities against the Asiatics, particularly those from the Old Kingdom.[38] We should add that these same inscriptions mention 'interpreters' (imy-r 'w) although the significance of this term is still under some discussion.[39] If we take this term to mean 'interpreters', as it appears to mean, it will imply the use of foreign labour by the Egyptians as early as the Old Kingdom. We find among the Sinai inscriptions from this period titles such as "controller of interpreters," "overseer of interpreters," "second-in-charge of interpreters," "overseer of interpreters," appearing in inscriptions 13, 16, 17 and 18.[40] We usually associate Asiatic workmen in Egypt with the Middle Kingdom. However, F. Debono has emphasized that the foreign tools and the proto-Sinaitic inscriptions suggest a considerable number of foreign workmen in the Sinai during the Old Kingdom.[41] This would not be so surprising if the foreign workers were local inhabitants in the area.

But there is some reason to think that Asiatic work-gangs were in Egypt during the Old Kingdom, as early as the fifth dynasty. In Egypt itself, apart from reliefs showing Asiatic prisoners in the early dynasties of the Old Kingdom, we have two clear examples showing Asiatic work-gangs being moved by ship, presumably from one place of work to another. They are from the reliefs of Sahure[42] and from the causeway of Unas[43] (see figs. 2 & 3). We discuss these particular scenes in detail in our chapter on Egyptian shipping. However, it is important to draw attention to them here in conjunction with the Sinai inscriptions of the Old Kingdom, particularly as we suggest they may have travelled to and from the Sinai by water along the Wadi Tumilat during this period (see map, fig. 4).

The texts and records of the early dynasties reveal considerable contact with Asiatic foreigners, no doubt through the area of the eastern Delta. During the Old Kingdom, we find titles such as "smiter-of-all-foreign (hill-)countries" attached to Sahure, Neuserre and Djedkare-Isesi, which may well refer to successes

Figure 2. From the pyramid temple of Sahure, fifth dynasty, come fragments of a number of boats, on board which are Asiatics, who are neither prisoners nor newly arrived in Egypt, for the reasons given in chapter six on Egyptian shipping. These reliefs show women and children among the group of Asiatics, accompanied by Egyptian interpreters. They seem to be work gangs being moved from one place of work to another.

Figure 3. This scene, similar to fig. 2, is from the Unas Causeway, also from the fifth dynasty. The many hogging-trusses show that these boats are for moving heavy cargo. The triangular object on the prow of one of the boats is an anchor (see end of chapter 6).

against the Asiatics in Lower Egypt only, and not necessarily any further afield.[44] We know that, under Pepi I, Uni made war on the Asiatic Sand-dwellers in their own lands, crossing their territory five times.[45] In order to get into their region, he had to cross over some water in boats with his men. He then marched them to the north of the Sand-dwellers, from which point he defeated them. Lest we take too literally the term ḥryw-šʿ (those-upon-the-sand) as signifying nomads, we should also emphasize that this text refers to the destruction of their fortresses and the cutting down of their vines and fig-trees, all of which suggest a settled population in a fertile region.

We have so far mentioned Sile as the gateway to the north. But there was another way into Asiatic territory for intermittent periods of time in Egypt's history. This was the Wadi Tumilat, a canal consisting of water from the Nile, which, branching off from the Pelusiac arm at the level of Saft el Henneh, flowed in the direction of Lake Timsah and Ismailiyah. This was, and still is, a natural depression which took the water of the inundation naturally into the Bitter Lakes. These lakes form part of another area which is low lying and will hold the water which flows into it. It is believed that at several stages in Egypt's history, the excess water in these areas flowed southwards from the Bitter Lakes into the Red Sea.

In his excellent study of the possibility of a canal running from the Nile into the Red Sea during Pharaonic times, Professor G. Posener stressed the geological evidence for the fact that the Wadi Tumilat was once a branch of the Nile, because black mud from the river has been found as far afield as the area around Ismailiyah.[46] There can be no doubt that this was once a natural waterway between the Nile and the Red Sea. Strabo tells us that "it was first cut by Sesostris before the Trojan War,"[47] a fact that would not exclude its having been a natural waterway before that time. Some scholars have believed that the waterway was in use at the time of Ramesses II. There are some grounds for thinking that it may have been in use at the time of Ramesses III, judging from the way in which the records describe the arrival of the foreign attackers. This idea is reinforced by the clear and indisputable statement in the historical section of the Papyrus Harris that the Egyptian copper mining expedition to Atika travelled by water, each way, in mnš boats. A glance at our map (fig. 4) will show that this way, though longer, must have been

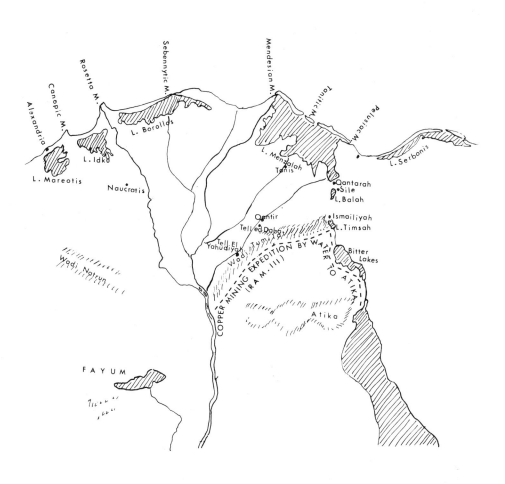

Figure 4. This map shows the various places mentioned in these chapters. The Wadi Tumilat is particularly important to the theory which this book puts forward, as the author believes it to be the route along which Egypt's attackers arrived, and also the route which the copper mining expedition from the time of Ramesses III took to reach Gebel Atika, since the Papyrus Harris tells us that they went there by water in mnš ships.

the easier way for them. We cannot imagine the existence of any other waterway to Atika. If we could only make some stratigraphical studies of the sites along the Wadi Tumilat and the related areas, we might, even at this late stage, gather some useful information. For example, we know that the harbour of Alexandria has sunk a number of feet into the sea. Yet in this case, the subsidence can only have occurred in classical times or later. The problem lies in dating these changes.

There can be no doubt at all that whenever there was water in the Wadi Tumilat, the Asiatics made full use of it to come westwards by boat. The Sinai inscriptions contain many references to travel by water in the Old Kingdom, but few for the Middle Kingdom.[48] The pictorial record from the Old Kingdom seems to confirm this as much as the texts.

Egyptologists have been unable to interpret completely and satisfactorily the reliefs in the proto-dynastic and early dynastic documents—palettes, mace-heads, vases and other objects— recording memorable events of those times, but there can be no doubt that the Asiatic figure was the enemy even then. Fortunately for us, we can recognise him clearly by his features, his beard and hair style and the weapons that he used, and sometimes by the associated symbols used by the Egyptian artist.

Both sides of the Narmer palette (figs. 5 and 6) show that the Asiatics had just been routed and we have here the earliest portrayal of an Egyptian ruler smiting an enemy with a mace.[49] It does not surprise us to see that the enemy is Asiatic. Above this man is another figure which has fascinated everyone for as long as the Narmer palette has been known. Before we go any further we must emphasize that this Asiatic is *not* being led by his nose, as the drawn reproductions of this relief have so often shown. In the original relief there is clearly a cord around his neck, which shows below the beard which goes back as far as his ears. The other Asiatic also has the remains of such a cord around his neck. (That is how Asiatic prisoners are always shown in captivity in Egypt.) Taking note of this cord around his neck, it then becomes clear that the first figure is meant to be understood as being pulled along by Horus as though he were a boat, which he no doubt symbolizes. This Asiatic is also shown to be coming through swampland from the east, a detail which would not have been lost on any Egyptian of that time, apart from the numerals

Figure 5. One side of the famous palette of Narmer. In the top right can be seen the Asiatic being led by Horus, not by his nose, but by a cord around his neck, like a boat. But he also represents an island. See W.A. Ward, "Supposed Asiatic Campaign of Narmer," *Mélanges de l'Univ. Saint Joseph*, XLV, Beirut, 1969 for a recent discussion of this object.

which this swamp plant is also meant to represent.[50] However, this 'boat' really consists of an 'island' sign in the Egyptian hieroglyphs, a fact that we cannot overlook. Can it be that we have here an Asiatic island dweller, who, because of the nature of his territory, had to move around in a boat? It is obvious that these two symbols are meant to characterise him clearly.

The nature of the Asiatic enemy is described in the Instruction for Meri-Ka-Re from which we have quoted before with reference to the Delta:

> . . . the wretched Asiatic—it goes ill with the place where he is, afflicted with water, difficult from many trees, the ways thereof painful because of the mountains. He does not dwell in a single place, but his legs. . . . He has been fighting since the time of Horus, (but) he does not conquer, nor yet can he be conquered. He does not announce a day in fighting. . . . The bowmen, however, are a locked wall, opened. . . . I made the Northland smite them, I captured their inhabitants and I took their cattle, to the disgust of the Asiatics against Egypt. . . . [51]

On the other side of the palette of Narmer (fig. 6) are ten headless corpses laid out in two rows, their heads placed neatly between their feet. On a higher register over them is shown a boat of "foreign" shape, that is, not papyriform or sickle-shaped, standing empty, again being pulled by a bird, possibly Horus. There is a door or a gate leading to the east which one feels is standing open. The boat is clearly the method of transport used for travelling to or from the east, while the heads of the dead men show that they are Asiatics by their beards and probably also by their caps, which are double-crowned.

It is a remarkable fact that they are shown to be wearing nothing on their bodies and that it is only the caps which must serve to identify them. Surprisingly, we see these same characteristics in another and much later document, a Megiddo ivory, dated by Dr. Loud to around 1350 B.C. although it was found in a stratigraphical level of around 1200 B.C. (fig. 7).[52] It is an ivory which Dr. Loud places with others in a Phoenician group, and which has often been reproduced for its interesting content. However, it is only recently that we have had the benefit of Dr. Raphael Giveon's study of the Shosu-Beduin,[53] which enables us to identify the two figures in the ivory as belonging to that group, by their characteristic head-gear. They too appear to be

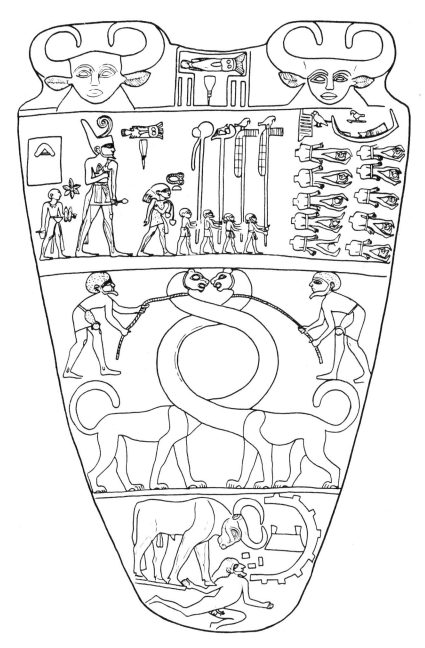

Figure 6. The other side of the well-known but little understood palette of Narmer, from early dynastic times. It is suggested in the chapter on the Delta that the ten headless men are Shosu-Beduin, and predecessors of the Sea Peoples, who came to Egypt by the same route and very likely for similar reasons.

wearing nothing on their bodies. Nearly three millennia later, a traveller, Gabriel Brémond, speaks of the Beduin as a completely naked people who lived from the trading of cattle and buffalo skins.[54] This ivory is particularly interesting to Egyptologists because it shows us Asiatics as prisoners of other Asiatics. We tend to forget that a great deal of destruction occurred in the Near East and the Aegean as much by wars and fighting among city states themselves, as by the action of Egyptian armies from the south or any "invaders" from the north.

But to return to our Shosu-Beduin. Dr. Giveon quotes a text, (Document 51, page 164), which clearly states that the Shosu-Beduin came to Egypt from the east, the exceptional determinative used in this case being a boat. This fits the facts as we see them very well indeed. Dr. Giveon, however, expressed some doubt about the correctness of the text since it is a late one from the Temple of Edfu (XXV-XXVI dynasties) even though its language has some archaic overtones.

Dr. Giveon's study of the Shosu-Beduin emphasizes that they appear in the records by that name only from the first half of the eighteenth dynasty and only until the time of Ramesses III. The documentary evidence places these people within a clearly defined geographical area, namely, the Delta, western Palestine, south-eastern Palestine, even though they also make an appearance in Syria. The term 'Shosu' appears to be a general term for a federation of tribes (mhwt), but also the name of a country, at least in the eighteenth dynasty, as Dr. Giveon shows in Document I.

It still remains a difficult problem to separate the various groups of Asiatics which we find mentioned in the documents of the Old Kingdom, and even in those of the Middle Kingdom, for the simple reason that the Egyptians did not refer to them in any but the most generic of terms. The reason for this is easy to understand: they did not know them very well themselves and there must have been only a few people in Egypt at any given time who could properly distinguish between the Asiatic groups. It is not until well into the eighteenth dynasty, after long contact with the Hyksos and presumably with other Asiatic groups, that we begin to find some distinctions being made by the Egyptians. Otherwise until quite late, they are 'Asiatics', 'foreign countries', 'Retenu', 'the lands or plains of the Fenkhu', 'Djahy', 'Kharu', none of these conveying to us any very clear geographical or ethnic definitions.

Figure 7. This well-known object, an ivory from Megiddo, is not yet properly understood. It shows two Shosu-Beduin as prisoners of another Asiatic group. Attention is drawn to their nakedness and their caps, which resemble those on the Narmer palette.

There are serious grounds for thinking that Retenu may have extended right into the eastern Delta and included some part of it from quite early times. Sir Alan H. Gardiner in his supplementary note on Retenu[56] noted that the use of this term in the texts of the Middle Kingdom implied that it could not have been very far from the peninsula of Sinai. He drew attention to the fact that in the inscriptions of Serâbît el-Khâdem dating from the time of Ammenemes III-IV the Egyptian miners were assisted by Retenu people and particularly by "the brother of the prince of Retenu." He concluded that for the Middle Kingdom, the term 'Retenu' was used generically for both Palestine and Syria.

The term 'Djahy' seems to refer substantially to the same area as Retenu. Dr. Claude Vandersleyen, in his discussion of these terms[57] emphasized that 'Djahy' was used for a region and not for a people. The people of Djahy were the Retenu. He too, recalling Herodotus,[58] agrees that from the way this term is used in the texts one is in Djahy immediately upon leaving the Nile Delta. Dr. Vandersleyen understands the term 'Djahy' to refer to all the Asiatic territory known to Egypt, rightly we believe.

We would go even further than this, to say that Retenu began where the various Asiatic settlements began, namely in the eastern Delta.

In the second Stela of Kamose we find that the Hyksos prince Apophis at Avaris is called "the ruler (ḥk3) of Retenu," even though he had been firmly established at Avaris, while the possessions of the defeated Hyksos are called "the good things of Retenu."[59]

The Papyrus Harris tells us that Ramesses III had built a temple in Nubia and another in Djahy,[60] suggesting that he had thereby offered this homage from each extreme of his kingdom. After the reference to the temple in Nubia, the Papyrus Harris says:

> I made for thee an august quarter in the city of the Northland, established as thy property forever. [Further on we find:] I built for thee a mysterious house in the land (t3) of Djahy, like the horizon of heaven which is in the sky, (named) "The House of Ramesses-Ruler-of-Heliopolis" . . . in Pekanaan as the property of thy name. I fashioned thy great statue resting in the midst of it (named) Amon of Ramesses ruler of Heliopolis. . . . The Asiatics of Retenu came to it, for it was divine.[61]

We believe that both the quotations given above refer to the same place, which must be in the Delta. The well-known Egyptian characteristic of caring for their temples and their gods was known not to have been shared by the Asiatics, and it is unthinkable that a temple of the kind described would have been built in foreign territory or in territory which might easily again have fallen into Asiatic hands. The site of this temple may well have been Avaris, known to have been favoured by the Ramesside kings, and discussed by Dr. Habachi in a recent study.[62]

The eighteenth dynasty introduced the term ḫ3rw for the northern Asiatic area and from the time of Akhenaton, ḫ3rw and k3š are found contrasted in such a way as to justify the respective renderings of Syria and Nubia or Palestine and Nubia.[63] The term ḫ3rw also appears to include the Asiatic area in the eastern Delta. Gardiner said that Max Müller may well have been right in suggesting that Khor or Kharu extended as far as the Egyptian Delta. He quotes from Papyrus Anastasi III,[64] in which a high official is described as "king's envoy to the princes of the hill-countries of Khor starting from Sele to Iupa (perhaps Joppa)."

Yet some distinction must be made between the terms 'Retenu' and 'Kharu' or 'Khor'. In a stela of Amenophis II from Mît Raḥînah (Memphis) the list of prisoners taken comprises princes of Retenu numbering 144; brothers of princes, 179; Apiru, 3600; living Shosu 15,020; Khorians, 36,300; living Nugassians, 15,070.[65] Here a definite distinction is made between the princes of Retenu and the very numerous Khorians.

From the reign of Tuthmosis III the booty of Megiddo is listed with a distinction between the works of Kharu and the works of Djahy,[66] which we can equate with Retenu.

But turning again to the Papyrus Harris, we find some odd figures among its lists. The towns of Kharu listed, together with their cattle, are remarkably small in number and cannot possibly represent the whole area of Palestine and Syria from their numbers. In Plate 68a the towns of Egypt are listed as 160 in number whereas the towns of Kharu number only nine. In Plate 11, line 11, the towns of both Kharu and Kush number only nine. Similarly, in Plate 12b various cattle of the herds of Egypt number 847 while the various cattle of the lands of Kharu number only 19. Another example from Plate 69 compares the 961 cattle of

Egypt with the 19 animals representing the impost on the lands of Kharu.[67]

Such numbers must represent a very restricted area indeed and we believe they represent the area of the eastern Delta which had been brought under subjection by Egypt at this time. Otherwise these figures would contradict the numerous and frequent references to the abundant cattle and general produce of the lands of Djahy.[68]

It is with this more realistic picture of the Delta that we must approach the stela from the time of Sesostris III, found at Abydos and now in the Manchester Museum, giving us an account by Khu-Sebek (or Sebek-Khu), called Djaa, of an attack on the Asiatics in the north:

> His majesty proceeded northwards to overthrow the Asiatics (Mntyw-Stt).His majesty arrived at a region called Skmm. His majesty took the direction leading to the Residence of life, prosperity and health. Then Skmm fell, together with the wretched Retenu.[69]

The text has puzzled Egyptologists and it has been suggested that the lines have been written in the wrong order, or that perhaps a part of the text has been left out. While it is possible that this is so, it is also possible that it was meant to be taken just as it stands.

Bearing in mind the picture of the Delta which we believe the documents to present, it is enough for the Pharaoh simply to go northwards to arrive at the country of the Asiatics. The name of Skmm is most unlikely to stand for Schechem, as has been suggested. The sounds are entirely different and such suggestions have been misleading.

The Hyksos settlement in Egypt was not an isolated phenomenon. We are all familiar with the Admonitions of Ipuwer which John Van Seters, adducing good evidence,[70] believes should be dated around the thirteenth dynasty. Among other things the text says:

> The nomes are laid waste. A foreign tribe has come to Egypt . . . the Marshlands have become an open book to them (?). Lower Egypt is overrun (?) . . . the Asiatics are skilled in the arts of the Marshlands . . . the foreign countries have become Egyptian citizens everywhere. . . . [71]

In other words, the Asiatics who were at home in Lower Egypt and knew the marshlands which the Egyptians hardly knew at all, had extended their interests and were claiming equal rights with the Egyptians. These are the conditions in which, it seems, the Hyksos came to power.

The easy installation of the foreign "hill-countries" (Asiatic Hyksos) in the eastern Delta is more understandable if we take into consideration the fact that the Asiatics had had a foothold there previously. Van Seters makes this point in his book,[72] although he would accept the Asiatic presence there only from the First Intermediate Period.

Professor William A. Ward has in recent years discussed the connections between Egypt and the Aegean and the Near East during the First Intermediate Period,[73] deciding that the evidence is not nearly as conclusive as had been supposed.

Very valuable work has also been done by Miss Olga Tufnell in the dating of Egyptian scarabs which will throw a great deal of light on these relationships.[74]

No one would deny an early trade between Egypt and the Asiatic countries. Indeed one could not deny it owing to the presence of foreign materials such as ivory and silver in the very early dynasties. We have already referred to Dr. Hennessy's study of Palestinian pottery, showing its presence at Abydos from the first dynasty and possibly earlier.[75] This would prove trade, if not an actual Asiatic presence in Egypt.

Nevertheless, we have the ḥꜣw nbwt and the Fenkhu to account for from the earliest times. These will be discussed elsewhere.

The more we look at the problem of the Asiatics in Egypt the more we realize that the Hyksos in Avaris and the attacks of the "Sea Peoples" are only two of the better documented manifestations of an endemic problem. The so-called Sea Peoples are referred to in the texts many times as Asiatics and rebels and are declared to have been defeated on their own lands, their towns destroyed and their trees cut down, in the usual manner for Asiatic towns.

During the New Kingdom frequent excursions northwards by the Pharaoh and his armies and officials had enabled Egyptians to begin to know these areas better and consequently to begin to distinguish between the various groups of Asiatics and to call them by the names of their cities or by their ethnical names. Unfortunately we cannot recognise these groups by their more precise names. Our difficulties are probably made worse by the fact that the names are undoubtedly wrongly pronounced and adapted versions of the authentic Asiatic ones and therefore probably will not follow the accepted rules for Semitic sound changes. This more careful identification of foreigners was something new for Egypt, and a departure from its insular tradition, if we may call it this.

It is important to stress that Asiatic attacks on Egypt's frontier, wherever that was exactly, were not confined to the reigns of Merenptah and Ramesses III. There is textual evidence showing that this had happened in other reigns. In the time of Amenophis III, the son of Hapu, Amenhotep, was made overseer of the marshland "in order to keep the foreigners within their places."[76] He was overseer of the Great Green and as such, he closed the mouths of the Nile for all but the units of the King's navy (riverine, of course). A post of such importance as this is known to have been held by two Pharaohs in person, Ramesses I and Sethos I.[77] Neither of them is ever recorded as having sailed on any sea, although we know Sethos travelled overland to the Asiatic countries.

In the fragmentary record of the siege of Megiddo, Tuthmosis III refers to "the lands of the Fenkhu, who had begun to invade my boundaries,"[78] and again in the Hymn of Victory, Amon-Re speaks to Tuthmosis III saying: "I have made powerless the invaders who came before thee."[79]

A Vienna fragment of a block from the time of Horemheb, though badly broken, tells us that Asiatics had been crossing the boundaries of Egypt:

> . . . a few of the Asiatics who knew not how to live, have come . . . after the manner of your father's fathers since the beginning. . . . Now the Pharaoh . . . gives them into your hand to protect their borders.[80]

A Karnak relief from the time of Sethos I calls him "the King who protects Egypt."[81] He is told: "They that transgress thy boundaries are bound."[81] There are many references to the Egyptian boundary in the texts from the reign of this Pharaoh.

When the Aswan Stela tells us that Ramesses II has extended Egypt's boundaries "forever," plundering the Asiatics (S̲t̲tyw) and capturing their cities, we must not exclude the possibility that he had, on this occasion, won for Egypt a part of the Delta. This is suggested by the text which says, using Gardiner's translation:

"He destroyed the warriors of the Great Green and Lower Egypt spends the night sleeping (peacefully)."[83]

It is clear that at this point we must turn our attention to the problem of the Great Green.

NOTES ON CHAPTER TWO

The following abbreviated references are used in this chapter:

Adams   R.M. Adams, *Land Behind Baghdad* (Chicago, 1965).

Breasted   J. Breasted, *Ancient Records of Egypt* (Chicago, 1906).

Erichsen   W. Erichsen, *Papyrus Harris I, Hieroglyphische Transkription* (Brussels, 1933).

Gardiner   A.H. Gardiner, *Ancient Egyptian Onomastica* (Oxford, 1947).

Gardiner   A.H. Gardiner and T.E. Peet, ed. J. Černý, *The Inscriptions*
and Peet   *of Sinai* (London, 1952-55).

Griffiths   J. Gwyn Griffiths, "Hecataeus and Herodotus on 'A Gift of the River'," *JNES*, (1966).

Hennessy   J.B. Hennessy, *The Foreign Relations of Palestine during the Early Bronze Age* (London, 1967).

Kees   H. Kees, *Ancient Egypt, A Cultural Topography* (Chicago, 1961).

Sethe, *Urk. I*   K. Sethe, *Urkunden des alten Reiches* (Leipzig, 1903).

Sethe, *Urk. IV* K. Sethe, *Urkunden der 18. Dynastie* (Leipzig, 1906-).

Thompson   K. Thompson and J. Gaudet, *A Review of Papyrus and its Role*
and Gaudet   *Role in Tropical Swamps* (1972) for *Archiv für Hydrobiologie.*

Vandersleyen   C. Vandersleyen, *Les guerres d'Amosis* (Brussels, 1971).

Van Seters   J. Van Seters, *The Hyksos* (New Haven, 1966).

Vercoutter   J. Vercoutter, "Les Haou-nebout," *BIFAO*, XLVIII (1949).

Wilson   J.A. Wilson, trans., in J.B. Pritchard, ed., *Ancient Near Eastern Texts Relating to the Old Testament* (Princeton, 1969³).

1. Vercoutter, pp. 108ff.; E. Uphill, "The Nine Bows," *JEOL*, Deel VI (1967): 393ff.

2. J.E. Quibell, *Hierakonpolis* (London, 1900), part I, plates XXV and XXVIc.

3. C.M. Firth, J.E. Quibell and J.P. Lauer, *The Step Pyramid* (Cairo, 1935), vol. II, plate 58.

4. Vercoutter, pp. 108ff.

5. Vercoutter, pp. 111f.

6. Vercoutter, pp. 114, VII.

7. J. Simons, *Handbook for the Study of Egyptian Topographical Lists Relating to Western Asia* (Leiden, 1937), pp. 4f.

8. Oriental Institute, University of Chicago, *Medinet Habu*, 1930-70, vol. I, plate 43; also W.F. Edgerton and J.A. Wilson, *Historical Records of Ramesses III* (Chicago, 1936), pp. 44f.

9. There is considerable hesitation about identifying Tenep and Yerteg and I can offer no suggestions.

10. Vercoutter, pp. 115, X.

11. J. Černý, "Reference to Blood Brotherhood among Semites in an Egyptian Text of the Ramesside Period," *JNES*, 14 (1955): 161ff.; also A.H. Gardiner and J. Černý, *Hieratic Ostraca* (Oxford, 1957), plate 78.

12. Griffiths, pp. 57f.

13. Griffiths, pp. 59f.

14. H.E. Hurst, *The Nile* (London, 1952), pp. 37f.

15. Strabo 17.I.3.

16. Adams, pp. 7f.

17. Adams, pp. 8f.

18. Adams, pp. 10f.

19. Finance Ministry, Survey Department of Egypt, *The Physiography of the River Nile and its Basin* (Cairo, 1906), pp. 336f.

20. Kees, pp. 52f. and pp. 185f.

21. Kees, pp. 55f.

22. Thompson and Gaudet.

23. Thompson and Gaudet, pp. 2f. and pp. 12f.

24. K. Thompson, *A report on the interactions between environmental factors and aquatic and semi-aquatic plants in the Okavango Delta, with recommendations for further lines of investigation* (1973), prepared for Project BOT/506, UN/FAO Land and Water Development Division, pp. 51f.

25. Herodotus II, 93.

26. Kees, p. 185.

27. Kees, p. 186.

28. Kees, p. 188.

29. Strabo 17.I.3.

30. Wilson, p. 417.

31. J. Couyat and P. Montet, *Les inscriptions hiéroglyphiques et hiératiques du Ouadi Hammâmât*, Mém. Inst. Fr.34 (1912), No. 192, inscription of vizir Amenemhet, last two lines; also Breasted, vol. I, par. 453.

32. Gardiner, vol. II, p. 203*.

33. Kees, pp. 190f.

34. J.B. Pritchard, *The Ancient Near East in Pictures* (Princeton, 1954), plate 326; see also A.H. Gardiner, *JEA* 6 (1919): 99f.

35. Wilson, pp. 417f.

36. M. Bietak, "Vorläufiger Bericht über die dritte Kampagne der österreichischen Ausgrabungen auf Tell ed-Dabʿa im Ostdelta Ägyptens (1968)," *MDIAK*, 26 (1970): 15ff.

37. See Hennessy; also M. Chéhab, "Relations entre l'Egypte et la Phénicie des origines à Ounamon," *The Role of the Phoenicians in the Interaction of Mediterranean Civilizations*, ed. W.A. Ward (Beirut, 1968).

38. J. Černý, "Semites in Egyptian Mining Expeditions to Sinai," *Archiv Orientalni*, VII (1935): 384ff.

39. On ỉmy-r ʿw see H. Goedicke, *JEA*, 46 (1960): 60f. as well as R.O. Faulkner, "Egyptian Military Organization"in *JEA*, 39 (1953): 34f.

40. Gardiner and Peet, vol. II, pp. 12f.; also J. Van Seters, "A Date for the 'Admonitions' ", *JEA* (1964): 20ff. and W. Hayes, *A Payrus of the Late Middle Kingdom in the Brooklyn Museum* (1955), pp. 92ff.

41. F. Debono, "Pics en pierre de Sérabit El Khadim (Sinai) et d'Egypte," *Ann. Serv.* 46 (1947): 281ff.

42. L. Borchardt, *Das Grabdenkmal des Königs Sahure* (Leipzig, 1913) Band II, Blatt 30.

43. S. Hassan, "The Causeway of Wnis at Sakkara," *ZAS*, 80, (1944): 139; also G. Goyon, *BIFAO*, 69 (1971): 3ff.

44. The fact that such titles as these were not automatically attached to all the records of all the Pharaohs is significant.

45. Sethe, *Urk. I*, pp. 104f.; also Breasted, vol. I, pars. 314f.

46. G. Posener, "Le canal du Nil à la Mer Rouge avant les Ptolomées; *Chronique d'Egypte*, 13 (1938): 259ff.

47. Strabo 17.I.25.

48. Gardiner and Peet, pp. 14ff.

49. W.M. Flinders Petrie, *Ceremonial Slate Palettes* (London, 1953), plates J and K.

50. L. Keimer, "Bemerkungen zur Schiefertafel von Hierakonpolis," *Aegyptus* VII (1926): 169ff.

51. Wilson, pp. 416f.

52. G. Loud, *The Megiddo Ivories*, Oriental Institute, University of Chicago, 1939, plate 4, 2a and b.

53. R. Giveon, *Les Bédouins Shosu des documents égyptiens* (Leiden, 1971); also, "The Shosu of the late XXth Dynasty," *JARCE* 8 (1969-70): 51ff.

54. Gabriel Brémond, *Voyage en Egypte de 1643-1645*, ed. J.C. Goyon (Cairo, 1974), p. 19.

55. Vandersleyen; W. Helck, *Die Beziehungen Aegyptens zu Vorderasien im 3. und 2. Jahrtausend v. Chr.* (Wiesbaden, 1971²); Van Seters; Gardiner.

56. Gardiner, vol. I, p. 142*.

57. Vandersleyen, pp. 90ff.

58. Vandersleyen, pp. 95f.

59. L. Habachi, *The Second Stela of Kamose* (Glückstadt, 1972), pp. 37f., see also M. Hammad, "Découverte d'une Stele du Roi Kamose," *Chronique d'Egypte*, 30 (1955): 198ff., particularly 205.

60. W. Erichsen, *Papyrus Harris I, Hieroglyphische Transkription* (Brussels, 1933), I, 8,2f. and I, 9, 1f.

61. Breasted, vol. IV, pars. 215ff.

62. L. Habachi, "Sethos I's Devotion to Seth and Avaris," *ZAS*, 100, (1974): 95ff.

63. Gardiner, vol. I, p. 180*.

64. Gardiner, vol. I, p. 183*.

65. Pritchard, pp. 245ff.

66. Van Seters, pp. 186f.

67. Erichsen, I, 68a; I,11,11; I, 12b; I, 69, 10; also corresponding plates in Breasted, vol. IV.

68. Vandersleyen, pp. 99f.

69. T. Eric Peet, *The Stela of Sebek-Khu* (Manchester, 1914).

70. Van Seters, pp. 116f.

71. A.H. Gardiner, *The Admonitions of an Egyptian Sage* (Leipzig, 1909), pp. 9f.

72. Van Seters, pp. 101f.

73. William A. Ward, *Egypt and the East Mediterranean World 2200-1900* B.C. (Beirut, 1971). Particularly important to our case is his chapter on Asiatics and the Delta. Although we believe that his picture of the Delta, geographically and politically, is not a realistic one, his material is important and his work is a valuable contribution in throwing light upon these problems.

74. O. Tufnell, "Hyksos Scarabs from Canaan," *Anatolian Studies 6*, (1956): 67ff.; also recent work on a dating method for Egyptian scarabs, publication forthcoming.

75. Hennessy, pp. 34f.

76. Cairo Statue 583, see W. Helck, "Der Einfluss der Militärführer in der 18. ägyptischen Dynastie," *Untersuchungen* 14 (Leipzig, 1939): 22f.

77. H. Kees, *Handbuch des Altertumwissenschafts des alten Orients* III, I.3 (München, 1933), pp. 109f.

78. Breasted, vol. II, par. 439.

79. Sethe, *Urk. IV*, p. 614; also Breasted, vol. II, par. 657.

80. Breasted, vol. III, par. 11; also Breasted, *ZAS* 38, 47.

81. Breasted, vol. III, par. 84.

82. Breasted, vol. III, par. 107.

83. Gardiner, vol. I, p. 195*.

The Great Green, the Islands and the ḥȝw nbwt

One of the most unfortunate conclusions arrived at by the early Egyptologists attempting to make sense of the Ramesside documents was that wȝḏ-wr "Great Green" meant 'sea'. This was a fundamental error that led scholars astray on other issues as well.

Among the factors contributing to the misunderstanding of this expression was the false analogy with the Semitic term for Mediterranean, 'the great ym'. But the use of the Semitic word ym, which may refer to any stretch of water, came into use in the Egyptian language only in the New Kingdom, after the Asiatic Hyksos presence in Egypt, while the Egyptian expression "Great Green" goes back to the earliest texts from the Pyramids.

Another factor which contributed to this error was the early publication and translation of the texts concerning the attacks on Egypt during the reigns of Merenptah and Ramesses III. Champollion himself recognised the Philistines in the Peleset of these records, a conclusion so probable that no one has ever questioned it.[1] It then became urgent to recognise Egypt's other attackers and on the mere basis of the similarity of the sounds of their names, assumptions were made by many scholars which required the attackers to come from the sea. Hence the confirmation of an error that has prevailed until today.[2]

If we examine the use of the expression "Great Green" in the Egyptian texts of any period, we find that it never indisputably means 'sea' from its context. Many examples of the use of this term may be found in the Erman *Wörterbuch* and in H. Gauthier's

Dictionnaire des Noms Géographiques,[3] and although the meaning given is always 'sea' with two minor exceptions in the *Wörterbuch,* there is not a single context where this is not an assumption rather than what the text itself demands.

In the Pyramid Texts, the expression "Great Green" is used a number of times and it is written sometimes with the canal determinative, sometimes with an oval sign, which we shall discuss later, and sometimes with no determinative at all.[4] The word meaning 'green' (w3d) is written either with the papyrus stem alone, or with the addition of the snake denoting the final sound of the word. There can be no doubt that originally, at least, this expression must have referred to fresh, inland water because of the vegetation which it implied. If "Great Green" originally referred to stretches of papyrus, then its meaning would denote swampland and essentially undrained areas, because we now know that papyrus will not grow where the level of the water changes very much or where there is fast flowing water.[5]

The notoriously difficult Pyramid texts cannot produce any context where "Great Green" must mean 'sea'. According to the now established custom, the instances where this expression has been used have been translated as 'sea' and 'ocean', but there appears to be no justification for this, nor do the texts make any sense when translated in this way. In two cases, we can make much better sense of the context if we abandon the accepted interpretation for a more literal one. In Utterance 484, section 1022, we find "Great Green" mentioned in conjunction with the mound appearing in the midst of the water, obviously a reference to the inundation and not to any sea or ocean.[6] Similarly in Utterance 437, 802a and b, there is a comparison of the winding watercourse in the northern heavens with a star crossing the Great Green. There is no point at all in this comparison if the winding river in the sky, presumably with vegetation along its banks, is not in some way similar to the Great Green.[7]

I suggested in 1972 that w3d-wr seemed to refer to a part of the Delta, judging from the way it was used in the texts of the Ramesside period, and earlier.[8] I am delighted to say that Dr. Claude Vandersleyen has taken up my plea to discover the actual meaning of w3d-wr, starting from the fact that it does not mean 'sea' or 'ocean'. We are looking forward to his published results in the near future.[9]

It is not possible to argue, as some have attempted to do, that the Great Green means 'sea' because its expanse looked green to the Egyptians. Vegetables and vegetation were 'green' to the Egyptians and the term conveyed to them also everything that was fruitful, vigorous, young and new. The texts never suggest confusion between 'green' and 'blue'.

The Abydos decree of Sethos I refers to the Great Green in several places, among them: "The lake in front of it (the Residence) is like the Great Green whose . . . is not known, when one gazes upon it bright like the colour of lapis lazuli, its middle part of papyrus and reeds, lilies abounding daily. . . . [10] Here the water of the lake is clearly referred to as being blue, while the fresh water and vegetation combined are likened to the Great Green.

In his lexicographical study of some ancient Egyptian paints and pigments, Erik Iversen defined w3d 'green' as meaning both 'green' and 'blue', green being used "as an ordinary colour adjective with the common and well-established meaning, 'green'.[11] Very oddly, when he comes to define this term as 'blue', he says that it is apparently used for "certain blue-green nuances which we should consider blue." He can offer no better example for this than the dubious colour of the vein as seen through the skin,[12] and he himself suggests that it is a questionable point whether it should be translated 'green' or 'blue' "as, for example . . . the sea." We see, therefore, that this is a circular argument.

One ought to add that the use by the ancient Egyptians of the term 'green' for whatever is fresh and vigorous is not yet sufficiently accepted by many readers who tend to interpret "green lips" as sickly rather than full and vigorous, and a "green face" as produced by an illness rather than by good health. Yet Professor Hermann Kees had given us, as far back as 1943,[13] a clear basis for a fresh approach to the interpretation of this colour, as well as others, in the ancient texts. In this as yet unsurpassed study, Kees not only stressed the meaning that w3d has of 'fresh', 'young' or 'radiant', but also that the meaning of the word was closely linked with the papyrus sign which is used for it.

Moreover, Kees's profoundly scholarly approach led him to point out[14] that "Great Green" translated as 'sea' remained an inexplicable phenomenon.

This view is confirmed by an examination of the pictorial

representations of the Great Green which are to be found.

In two Old Kingdom illustrations of the Great Green, from the fifth dynasty, we find it symbolised by a male fertility god, among other figures of plenty. From the tomb of Sahure, the Great Green is found in a row of figures including the god of corn, Nepri.[15] The body of w3ḏ-wr is covered with the wavy lines used by the Egyptians to denote water; all figures in this row seem to be associated with Lower Egypt (fig. 8). The Great Green is similarly portrayed in the tomb of Neuserre (fig. 9).[16] He is also to be found on the façade of the Sesostris I shrine at Karnak (fig. 10).[17] Representations of the Great Green are seen again, but bearing the fruits of the earth this time, on the walls of the Mortuary Temple of Ramesses III at Medinet Habu (Plates II & III).[18]

Perhaps the most important pictorial representation of the Great Green comes from Deir El-Bahari, where we may be surprised to find it on a list of the nomes of the Delta, one of the earliest lists we have (fig. 11).[19] In this list comprising Mendes, Heliopolis, Saïs and Athribis, we find w3ḏ-wr, km-wr, and šn-wr. Taken in this context it is clear that these three areas were not seas but nomes or divisions of governed Egyptian territory.

Professor W. Kelly Simpson remarked that the practice of representing the nomes of Upper and Lower Egypt and the estates within them as corpulent offering-bearers or as female servants advancing toward the King has a long history of development in the Old Kingdom pyramid and valley temples.[20] Simpson also emphasized that, associated with the nomes and their estates at this period and later, are other figures labelled w3ḏ-wr, Ḥaʿpy 'the inundation', Nepri (the grain god), Sekhet (the field goddess), and the seasons.[21]

The most artistically satisfying portrayal of the Great Green comes from the Book of the Dead of Ani (XIX dynasty) from the British Museum (Plate IV).[22] We may recall that Chapter 17 of the Book of the Dead in all cases refers to "Great Green," but the text, being religious or "magical," is not very clear to us. In the Book of the Dead of Ani we actually have a pictorial representation of the Great Green mentioned in the text. The figure, sitting down on the left is shown with the emblem of endless years in his right hand and on his head. Wavy lines clearly representing water are drawn carefully all over his body, which is painted an unmistakable blue in the original papyrus. This colour is not authentic

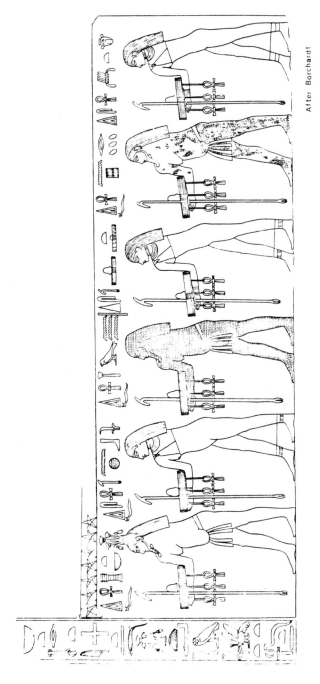

After Borchardt

Figure 8. From the tomb of Sahure comes this beautifully drawn w3ḏ-wr, shown in proximity to the corn god, Nepri, and other fertility figures closely associated with the Delta.

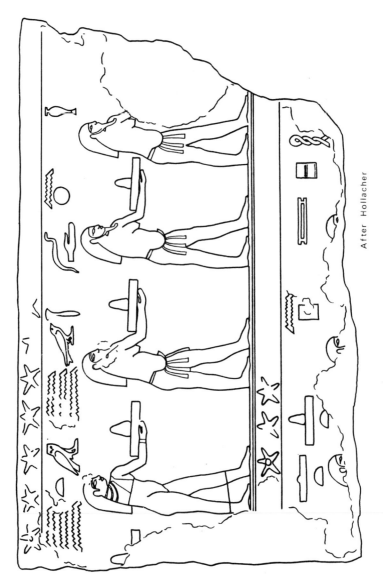

Figure 9. A portrayal of w3ḏ-wr from one of the chambers in the tomb of Neuserre, of the fifth dynasty.

After Hollacher

After Lacau and Février

Figure 10. Another representation, in a more formal context, of w3d-wr from the shrine of Sesostris I at Karnak.

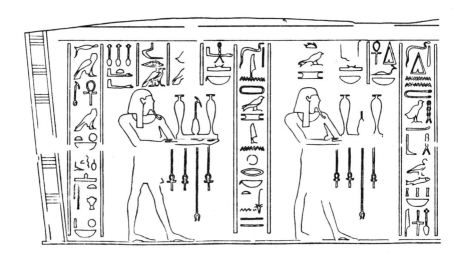

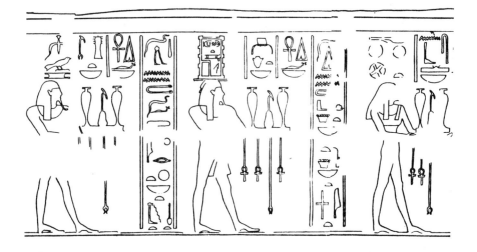

Sections 1 and 2 of figure 11.

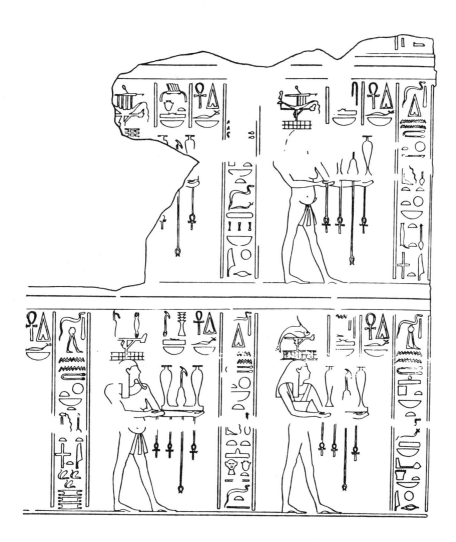

Section 3 of figure 11.

Figure 11. This important list of nomes from Deir El Bahari is one of the earliest. It includes, surprisingly, w3ḏ-wr, šn-wr and km-wr.

in British Museum Plate 8, dating to 1890, yet we must still consider this a beautiful publication. Although the name of the god Ḥeḥ has ended up being written next to the Great Green, there can be no doubt that the name is not intended to be attached to him, because he does not have the characteristics of Ḥeḥ beyond carrying the endless years signs in his hand and on his head.[23] The text speaks of two lakes, the lake of Maāt and the lake of Natron of endless years. This figure which we believe without any doubt to be the Great Green may have been associated in the mind of the scribe with those figures representing personifications of seasons as described in the study of Simpson which we have mentioned above.

Another reference to the Great Green which has a seasonal implication is in a text on British Museum Stela No. 138.[24] Here there is a reference to limbs which become like the serpent Apophis at the beginning of the year, when he is engulfed, head downwards, into the Great Green which "hides bodies."

Another such reference is to found among the maxims of Ani[25] in which the author, E. Suys, brings to our attention the use of "Great Green" in the plural, when the text speaks of the course of the water from the previous year which had taken another direction, the Great Green (plural) having dried out.

But the Egyptian historical documents are very clear in their references to the Great Green. When they refer to the Great Green, it is as though they are referring to a definite area, not an indefinite one.

In a study of military leadership in eighteenth dynasty Egypt, Professor H. W. Helck quotes from the Statue Cairo 583 vs line 14,[26] in which defence activity is described on the mouths of the Nile and the surrounding district, the area being closed to all except sailors. He cites a case of a "commander of the fortress of the Great Green" receiving tribute from the "foreign countries." The same commander also had the title of "fortress commander of the northern countries," which title, as we have already suggested in our previous chapter, could well refer to the Asiatics who were installed in Lower Egypt.[27]

Another title related to the one above is quoted by Gardiner from the Bilgai Stela: "a deputy of the fortress commander of the Great Green."[28] In these titles, the expression is used as the name of an area worthy of a fortress, an overseer and a deputy overseer.

We find too the title "chief of the record-keepers of the house of Great Green," referring to an administrative building there.[29]

From the time of Tuthmosis III we have "overseer of every river-mouth of the Great Green."[30] In the eighteenth dynasty titles such as "overseer of the river-mouths" and "overseer of the river-mouths of the hinterland" are to be found.[31] These suggest a vigorous attempt on the part of the Pharaonic administration to control these areas, which remain nevertheless so foreign to Egypt that they can only be referred to by such vague names. It is interesting to note that the "overseer of the river-mouths of the hinterland" was also "fortress commander of Sile" as is stated in the Stela of the Year 400.[32]

The Abydos decree of Sethos I refers to the many boats covering the Great Green and the river-mouths, with their freights of "drug-herbs of God's Land."[33] Here too the Great Green is associated with abundance and fertility in proximity to the mouths of the Nile. W. F. Edgerton and J. A. Wilson underline the fact that in Greek times, religious and offering texts speak of the mouths of the Nile (r3-ḥ3wt) as districts from which the inundation comes, and consequently also the fruits of the earth.[34]

It is important to emphasize that the references in the Egyptian texts to the water of the Nile flowing into the Great Green ought to be taken absolutely literally. We have already said that the Nile does not flow into the sea like other rivers. As far as the Egyptians were concerned, the Nile river flowed into the Delta, and *disappeared* there, the Delta being largely foreign territory. For this reason, the texts such as we find in *Urkunden* IV, 118 and *Urkunden* II, 16[35] should be reconsidered in the light of there not being any examples where "Great Green" indisputably means sea from its context. These passages suggest that the Great Green was a part of the Delta only.

Much has been made of the story of the Shipwrecked Sailor as proof that w3ḏ-wr in this case, at least, signified *sea*. But the point must be made, as forcefully as possible, that when the inundation was at its height, and in years when the Nile ran high, the Delta must have been a very dangerous place indeed in areas where the currents were strong with the full weight of the water behind them. The texts carry a number of references of disasters on the river and on the Great Green. Moreover, no one has yet understood exactly the passage which relates how the boat, in which the Shipwrecked Sailor was travelling, capsized. It is usually translated as having been a wave or an unexpected body of water. However, the shipwreck is not the main theme, only a part of the credible framework of the fairy story, as I have emphasized in a recent article in *Göttinger Miszellen* 16 (1975). Sudden winds were, and still are, common in the Delta, and in the time of the inundation would be very dangerous.

The only time that an Egyptologist has looked critically at the term we are discussing was in 1857 when Samuel Birch wrote a paper which appeared in French discussing the Egyptian inscription on a gold bowl from the time of Tuthmosis III which is in the Louvre. In this paper he discussed the titles given to the officer Toth to whom the bowl is dedicated. Among these titles we find: "the overseer of the foreign countries; the trusted man of the King in God's Land; the commander of the army; the garrison commander; he who fills the storehouses with lapis lazuli, silver and gold." Most important of all for the discussion was "the trusted man of the King in every foreign country and the islands which are in the midst of the Great Green."[36] Not surprisingly, most of the paper was dedicated to a discussion of the Great Green.

To be fair, Samuel Birch recognised the importance of the papyrus stem determinative in the writing of the expression and he took the trouble to point out that it normally had the value of 'pond' or 'lake'.[37] But unfortunately, the reference to 'islands' seemed to make it necessary that "Great Green" should mean 'sea' and, more particularly, the Mediterranean. Pressure from too many other scholars of the day decided matters for the worse.

The few times where the sea is certainly referred to in the Egyptian texts occur in the New Kingdom and in those cases the Semitic word ym is always used. In the story of Wenamun, we find the Mediterranean referred to as "the great ym of Kharu,"[38] and the word ym is used in a papyrus which speaks of the Asiatic goddess of the seas, Astarte.[39]

But when used in the Egyptian texts, ym does not always mean sea. More often it refers to an inland water, as we see from its use for the ym of Coptos and the Fayum, which simply means, 'the water'.[40]

In the texts concerning the Sea Peoples at Medinet Habu, the Turush and the Sherden are said to be "of the ym"[41] and in Papyrus Harris the Sherden and Weshesh are so defined.[42] In the earlier texts from the time of Merenptah, the Ekwesh are said to be "of the hill-countries of the ym."[43]

It is possible that ym may mean 'sea' in this context. We are well aware from the Amarna Letters that the western Asiatic city states had fleets of ships which engaged in piracy along the coast.[44]

But it is far more likely that the expression is referring here to inland waters, namely, the area of the Bitter Lakes. We pointed out in our previous chapter on the Delta that the eastern sector showed definite signs of being Asiatic and hostile to the Pharaoh. After looking at the evidence for this, still in a very fragmentary state, but nevertheless significant, we cannot rule out the likelihood that the hill-countries of the ym are those groups of Asiatics who had settled in the eastern Delta and the area around the Bitter Lakes and who periodically forced their way into Egypt by boat along the Wadi Tumilat, whenever there was enough water in it, or overland.[45] Owing to the lack of a modern survey of this area and the lack of a sufficient number of stratified sites in the vicinity, we do not yet have enough information on which to base any firm conclusions.

When the Asiatics are mentioned in the Egyptian texts, they always have as their determinative the hill-country sign, and there is good reason to think that this did not change after they settled in the eastern Delta area. The arguments for the quick assimilation of Asiatics living in Egypt are never very convincing, because they do not take into account the very profound differences in culture and outlook between Egypt and the various Asiatic groups who came or were brought in, by no means homogeneous societies.[46] Assimilation of Asiatic workmen may have been faster in Egypt proper than in the eastern Delta, where contact with the northern countries was continuous and the feeling often hostile, as we see from the records.

The view that ym means 'an inland water' in the texts relating to the Sea Peoples is reinforced by the fact that the Sherden have also been referred to as being "of the Great Green"[47] in Papyrus Anastasi II. As we have already said, "Great Green" never means 'sea' from the context of any passage in the Egyptian records.

Such an error was encouraged by the fact that 'islands' are very often mentioned in association with this term. Heinrich Brugsch was the only scholar who resisted the idea prevalent among the early Egyptologists that these islands were in the

Mediterranean and he suggested that *the islands of the Great Green* were islands formed by the Nile streams in the Delta.[48] He saw clearly in 1879 what we can now confirm from the greater number of texts that we have today that there is not a single reference to any island outside the Nile in the Egyptian texts before Wena-mun, unless we forcibly interpret a text in this way.[49]

If we are right in affirming that there is absolutely no evidence that w3ḏ-wr means 'sea', the argument that "the islands of the Great Green" refer to islands in the Mediterranean is no longer tenable.

The Islands

Every student of Egyptology is taught that there is no determinative indicating 'island'. Yet there is some evidence suggesting that this may not be right. The sign for the noun 'island', îw, called by Gardiner "the sandy tract" sign, is to be distinguished from the flatter 'earth' or 'land' sign for t3 and also from the oval representing the determinative for round as in the word 'circuit', Gardiner's sign Z 8 in his *Grammar.* To make matters more complicated, this same shape may be the deter-minative for 'loaf' as well.[50]

But in practice there is some confusion among these signs. If we look at the oval sign, which goes back to the earliest texts, it becomes clear that it is used very often with the names of Egypt's enemies. In a study by Dr. M. C. Kuentz in 1947, a great number of names of foreigners and enemies were found to be written with this determinative after their names.[51] This applied also to a number of Nine Bows, including Libya. Dr. Kuentz even went so far as to say that the early dynastic figure on the Palette of Narmer (our fig. 5), who is being pulled along by a rope by Horus, in fact personifies, in the oval sign, all the enemies surrounding Egypt. There can be no doubt that there is considerable logic in this idea, conceived before our suggestion that the Delta was foreign territory for Egypt. We have already stated our belief that this figure, portrayed in this particular way, personifies Egypt's Asiatic enemies by being both *island* and *boat* together. We have also already referred to the many Asiatic groups who not only lurked in the Delta, but settled there in patches of higher ground among the marshes and water. Hence the *islands.* It is no accident that we sometimes find this oval sign in the place of a hill-country sign, and vice versa, among the determinatives of

Egypt's enemies. This is clearly evident in the writing of the lists of the Nine Bows throughout the dynasties, which Vercoutter has set out with such clarity in his study.[52]

Dr. Kuentz found this oval sign very frequent in the Pyramid Texts. He found that even though the word for Libya was written there in a number of ways, the oval determinative was always the same.[53] Similarly this determinative was used in the ancient texts with "Great Green" and šn wr 'the great circle' (see fig. 12). Dr. Kuentz concluded that it was unlikely in these contexts to signify "a circle" but was a sign used by the Egyptians to indicate foreign land. We would not only agree with this, but would add that they did so because the main enemies, the northern countries, had always lived in the Delta as far as they could remember, and necessarily on islands. Thus the hill-country sign and the island sign became fused into one ethnic concept, which could be expressed by either sign. So strong was this idea that in actual practice the various similar signs also appear to mean 'island' at times, not surprisingly, we feel.[54]

The iww ḥryw-ib w3ḏ-wr, which Gardiner translated as "the middle islands of Great Green,"[55] we believe to be islands in the Nile Water of the Delta, which had some special significance to the Egyptians which is now lost to us. These were often distinguished from other islands and probably carried a special group of people. We have yet to find a home for the Sherden in the Delta.

It is with great delight that we are able to identify islands, in the Delta presumably, in the "Scorpion" mace-head relief, which is from pre-dynastic or early dynastic date (Plate VI).[56] Here four islands are shown in beautiful detail, at some distance from the papyrus swamp, which is placed north-west of the islands. At the damaged base of the mace-head and difficult to see at first is the remaining end of a "foreign-shaped" boat. The outline of its prow follows vertically the reed enclosure of the date palm. It is interesting that another such enclosure is shown on an island in another early dynastic object, a slate palette the pieces of which are shared between the British and the Ashmolean Museums.[57] Unfortunately, however, the top of the enclosure is damaged.

Similarly, from the Book of the Dead of Ani,[58] we have a drawing of islands in the world hereafter, which cannot be very different from the ones that the Egyptians saw on earth (Plate VII). Strangely enough, such islands are still in use in France

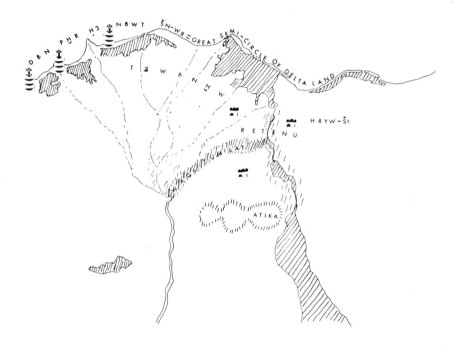

Figure 12. This is a map showing the suggestions made in the text. Not many people are expected to agree with it at first.

today, west of Arras, where, from the train, one can see people cultivating the islands or picking the harvest, by boat.

In his Commentary on the Wilbour Papyrus, Gardiner discussed the use of ïdb 'riparian land' and the expression ïw n m3wt, which he rendered as 'new land'.[59] Throughout the discussion, however, he shows a strong element of uncertainty.

There is no doubt that we need to continue to look closely at the use of all these terms in the texts in the hope of arriving at more satisfactory conclusions.

The ḥ3w nbwt

It is only because of the fundamental work done on the texts relating to the ḥ3w nbwt by Vercoutter,[60] and to the contributions made by Dr. Vandersleyen[61] and Dr. Uphill[62] as well as the earlier work by Pierre Montet and others,[63] that we are now able to refer briefly to this problem and make some suggestions towards a solution, from the standpoint that w3ḏ-wr does not mean 'sea'. It will not be possible to refer to all the prolific writing on this subject or to comment on all the work done on it.

Our greatest debt is to Vercoutter who studied this whole question in depth, putting this problem back in the setting in which it belongs: in the content of the Egyptian texts and in their use of this name. He has given us a standard work to which we shall always be able to refer with profit.

The problem of the identification of the ḥ3w nbwt has been clouded by late translations of this term as 'Greeks', but even allowing for a change in the application of this geographical term, the problem has remained obscure and hopeless at every level.

In examining this name and the people which it refers to, Vercoutter discussed the early readings of Golénischeff, Max Müller, Von Bissing and others.[64] Giving convincing reasons for his final decision, he concluded, as Gardiner did, that the name must be read ḥ3w nbwt, even taking into account the minor variations in the writing of the name throughout Egypt's history.

For the first part of the name, ḥ3w, Vercoutter accepted Gardiner's interpretation that it means 'around', or 'behind', or 'those who are around or behind', the nbwt.[65] The second part of the term still poses a difficult problem, although most scholars believe, from the way in which it is used in the texts, that it means some kind of island.

Kurt Sethe's view that nbwt was derived from the root nbỉ 'swim', was dismissed by Gardiner and also by Vercoutter on the grounds of common logic.[66] This is a verb of motion, so how could it possibly apply to islands in the sense of 'swimming' or 'moving' islands? Both scholars drew attention to the determinative of baskets which persisted without variation throughout the ages until the latest period.[67] Yet Sethe's idea assumes a fresh attraction in the light of some recent research by plant biologists in the ecology of papyrus.

We have already referred to the work of Thompson and Gaudet on papyrus.[68] They found that the papyrus swamp required fresh water, not fast flowing nor susceptible to much change in level. Consequently such growth would not be found near sea-water but only in areas which were safe from the intrusion of the sea.

Each underwater rhizome of papyrus, they found, produces one new shoot at a time, extending its horizontal growth in this way.[69] The life of each papyrus stem on the plant is about one hundred days, after which it droops over and lies on top of the underwater stems and root system, this whole underwater section of the plant being called 'sudd'. In this way light is allowed to reach the new stems above, while below there is a thickening tangle of dead papyrus stems which soon rises well above the water. The thickness of the 'sudd' is always shown in relation to papyrus in the Egyptian drawings, even in what is probably the first pictorial representation ever of papyrus, on the "Scorpion" mace-head, which can be seen in our Plate V.

In long-established swamps in Uganda, people are known to live on islands of papyrus. It is a well-known fact that areas of papyrus growth, up to one kilometre in diameter, may break off from the parent growth and actually float (or swim!) away. Hundreds of such islands have been known to occur in the one area.[70] One can imagine circumstances in which it might serve the island community "to cut themselves off" without necessarily waiting for natural causes to do it for them. Hence we find *swimming islands* a physical reality.

Moreover, the thickly matted dead papyrus stalks would look like baskets floating about on the water, if seen from a distance. If there were any people living on them, they would be the ỉmyw nbwt, to be distinguished from those who lived 'behind' or 'around' the nbwt, the ḥȝw nbwt.

There is, of course, no way we can prove that the nbwt consisted of papyrus. Yet there is a most interesting text quoted by Vercoutter in his study, a sarcophagus text, which says: "I am a w3d amulet which comes from the nbwt."[71] Here we find the w3d or papyrus amulet associated with the nbwt, whose inhabitants, another sarcophagus text tells us, were traders in semiprecious and precious stones.[72]

The name of h̲3w nbwt is to be found as early as the Pyramid Texts and also in inscriptions from the fourth and fifth dynasties.

We have already said that the Pyramid Texts are rarely very enlightening in their use of terms about which we would like to know more. Nevertheless we should see what they tell us about nbwt. In lines 628a to 629b, using Mercer's translation, we find:

> Thy two sisters Isis and Nephthys come to thee; they heal thee complete and great, in thy name of 'Great Black', fresh and great, in thy name of 'Great Green', behold, thou art great and round, like the 'Great Round', behold, thou art bent around and art round like the 'Circle which encircles the nbwt'.[73]
>
> [Lines 847a to 847c tell us:] Osiris . . . thou hast encircled every god in thine arms, their lands and all their possessions. Osiris . . . thou art great, thou art bent around the circle which encircles the nbwt.[74] [On a similar note are lines 1630c to 1631a:] Thy sister Isis laid hold of thee when she found thee, complete and great, in thy name of 'Great Black', encircle all things in thine arms in thy name of 'Circle which encircles the nbwt'.[75]

Vercoutter draws attention to the fact that one of the versions of this last-quoted text carries the oval sign as a determinative for nbwt.[76] But he is not convinced that this represents an island sign, even though he has considered the study of Dr. Kuentz which we referred to earlier, and which, we believe, shows fairly clearly that this determinative was used for foreign settlers and *did* mean island.[77]

From the fourth dynasty Montet drew attention to a re-used block found at Lisht in the pyramid of Ammenemes I, which carries the inscriptions: hwfw ft̲rrw , ph̲rw h̲3w nbwt and whmw h̲3w t3w.[78] This is a most interesting inscription to which we shall return later.

The funerary temple of Sahure (V dynasty) carries the inscription: "I bring for you the Iwntyw, the Mntyw, all the foreign countries and the h̲3w nbwt," a text which has been repeated many times in substance throughout Egypt's records.[79]

Most of the texts referring to the nbwt suggest they represent the outermost reaches of the earth, as the northern sea-coast must have appeared to the ancient Egyptians of all periods. This is to be seen in many of the texts quoted for us by Vercoutter, as for example his text XL, from the time of Ramesses III in a hymn to Amon, in which we are told that "the fear of him is in all the lands of the plains (t3w) because it is Amon who has made the ḥ3w nbwt. His terror has been placed in the Great Circle, for it is Amon who encircles the Nine Bows."[80]

Taking into account all the passages in which we can find references to the ḥ3w nbwt, their most striking association is with šn wr 'the Great Circle'. Earlier in this chapter we have already referred to the text from Deir El Bahari (our fig. 11) in which km wr, šn wr and w3d̲-wr are clearly portrayed as nomes, or at least recognised divisions, of the Delta.

The dbn pḥr ḥ3 nbwt 'the circle which turns around (embraces) the islands', has always been interpreted in a general and wide sense, almost as though it were a purely philosophical idea. Yet we believe this to be a precisely physical and geographical definition.

Recent research by Sneh and Weissbrod on a defunct Pelusiac branch of the Nile led to the recognition of some interesting general characteristics of the Delta, which have never been set out so clearly before.[81] Chief among these is the definition of "the strand plain which borders the deltaic plain in the north," consisting of "numerous bundles of very low accretional ridges." The width of this strand plain varies. It has been measured by these geologists in the easternmost sector of the Delta and found to range from one kilometre to twenty-five kilometres in width. This plain is sometimes broken up into a series of islands, which nevertheless run in the same direction. They found that the ridges, which were only a few tens of centimetres higher than their surroundings, can be followed along the coast for some kilometres. They also found that neither the minor tributaries of the Pelusiac branch of the Nile, which they were studying, nor the main branch, continued across the strand plain.

We cannot, of course, be sure that the shoreline was like this all the time in Egypt's ancient history. Yet it is clear that we have just described some characteristics of the area. One thing we can be sure of is that the shoreline of the Delta was semi-circular from the earliest times of its existence. This shape would no doubt be visible from the land on either side of the Delta or from a boat approaching or leaving the coast.

Consequently, the Great Circle may very well be the outermost semi-circle of the Delta, bordering on the sea. It is more likely to refer to the land limit, rather than to the sea itself. In a text from Edfu we find: "I bring for you the canal . . . whose volume fills the Great Circle. . . ."[82] Even if we take this to be an abstract idea, it must clearly have its origins in physical reality.

The link of the ḥ3w nbwt with the Great Green appears to be strong at all times, from the Pyramid Texts until ptolemaic times. We believe this associates them, beyond all doubt, with the Delta. We have already quoted passages from the Pyramid Texts showing this connection. As late as the reign of Nectanebo, we find the Naucratis Stela referring in line 9 to the "ḥ3w nbwt of the Great Green," while line 12 speaks of Neith as "mistress of the Great Green."[83]

Assuming that "Great Green" has not changed in meaning during this time and still refers to a part (or more?) of the Delta, and assuming that the "Great (Semi-) Circle" referred to the outermost shoreline of the Delta, we would have to place the ḥ3w nbwt in some area within these limits where swampland is likely to have existed.

We would not be opposing any of the evidence by placing them in the Delta, in the general area later occupied by the Greeks, who themselves also became "those who live around the nbwt" being so referred to from Year 3 of the reign of Amasis.[84] We believe we should treat ḥ3w nbwt as a purely geographical term. We have suggested several possibilities on our map (fig. 12), and we hope that further work and general discussion may help us to narrow down these possibilities even further. We cannot exclude any of the outer-lying lakes as possible sites, but we believe that the texts themselves, because they refer to them as Greeks in later times, indicate Lake Idku and Lake Mareotis more favourably than the others.

We have already made the distinction between "those who live in the nbwt" and "those who live behind or around the nbwt." But a distinction has yet to be made between the latter and the ḥ3w t3w, those who live around the plains, mentioned in the Khufu block and quoted earlier.[85] Again we believe that a literal meaning has to be sought. The "plains of the Fenkhu" are mentioned too early and too often in the Egyptian texts to be remote areas in Palestine and Syria.[86] We believe we have no choice but to place them in the Deltaic plains, their t3w shrinking to two only in later times, according to our texts. They too have been given a place on our map.

The ḥ3w nbwt seem always to merit a special mention in the Egyptian lists of enemies. In the Gebel Barkal Stela of Tuthmosis III we find: "I have bound in a sheaf the Nine Bows, the middle islands of the Great Green, the ḥ3w nbwt, the rebellious foreign lands."[87] This is only one of many such statements for all periods. We also find that these people usually head the list of Nine Bows written out in full.

Besides the one island determinative which Vercoutter found used with this name, and to which we have already referred, this scholar's chronological list of the writing of this name shows that, from the First Intermediate Period onwards the hill-country determinative is sometimes used with this name, most often in conjunction with the throwstick, signifying hostility towards Egypt. We have already stated our view that the Egyptians continued to call the foreign Asiatic settlers in the Delta by the general name of their original homeland, the "hill-countries." We cannot sufficiently emphasize that Egypt's insular attitude to her neighbors led her to refer to them by the vaguest of names. This was precisely because her geographical notions were severely bounded by physical barriers which were not entirely removed until Graeco-Roman times.

It should not surprise us, therefore, to find the Egyptians using the term ḥ3w nbwt for everyone who came from that area, regardless of the new factor that a large number of Greeks were now among the former inhabitants of the area. After all, the Delta had never been Egypt, and it had always been quite a triumph for the Pharaoh to subdue any of its nomes sufficiently to extract dues from them.

If the ḥ3w nbwt did live in the north-western Delta, we should find the texts confirming this. In a Ptolemaic text we find: "I have given to him the ḥ3w nbwt, they bring to him the channel-stream of the Great Green."[88] In an Edfu text we find "He brings for you the eight hnwt of Egypt through which Hapy 'the inundation' is taken to the ym which is behind the ḥ3w nbwt."[89] Here the use of ym could refer to the sea or to a lake. In another text from Edfu we have: "He brings you the ḥ3w nbwt of the Nine Bows, that is to say of the islands of the ym and of the many northern countries who live from the water of the stream channels."[90] In this context it would seem that ym does not mean 'sea' because the people from the northern countries are said to be living from the water of the stream channels. Such channels, as far as the Egyptians were concerned, could only be from the water of the Nile. No sense can be made of this text in any other way.

It is possible that the area which the ḥ3w nbwt may have inhabited was very productive. In the Instruction for Meri-Ka-Re we are told: "I pacified the entire west, as far as the coast of the Great Green. It works for itself as it gives meru-wood and one may see juniper."[91] Timber production was in keeping with the Asiatic tradition and may well have been one of the industries of those who lived around the nbwt, though such an environment could not provide the large and heavy trees of a mountain woodland.

We must reconsider all the terminology relating to the Asiatics, in fact, all the geographical terminology recorded in the Egyptian texts. For example, the pḥw nw Sttyw, which is always translated as "the ends of Asia" will yield very different results once we accept the fact that Asiatics were settled in the Delta. Consequently, the "marshes" of the Asiatics could be along any of the lakes in the north or the Bitter Lakes in the east.

The definitions of Naharin and Mitanni will have to be looked at again, fundamentally and from the standpoint of what the texts actually say. Naharin ought to be a geographical concept from its name, taken from the Hebrew *Nāhār*, 'river', as Gardiner pointed out.[92] It is thought that it refers to a geographical area which includes the political state of Mitanni. The Egyptian texts refer to the sons of the chiefs of Nahry in the tomb of Kenamun[93] and to a noble of Nahry in another eighteenth dynasty text,[94] while in the story of the doomed prince one of the chief characters is a prince of Naharin.[95] It is possible that the area referred to by Egypt as Naharin is not the same as the area referred to by that name by Anatolian and Western Asiatic scholars today. We have to allow for the possibility that places of similarly sounding names existed at the same time.

Naharin is often mentioned in the Egyptian texts and in such a way as to tempt us to believe that it was more likely to have been east of the Euphrates and in the general area of the Orontes, because it was more easily accessible to the Egyptians. It is even possible that the term 'Naharin' covered the area as far south as the eastern Delta.

Gardiner pointed out that Naharin is significantly absent from the list of enemies of Ramesses III in the inscription of year 8. We believe that this was because the Naharin area was hill-country territory, and Asiatic, and had joined the coalition against Egypt.

We have not made much progress in this question since Gardiner summarised it so ably in his *Onomastica*,[96] although Helck has added some valuable details to this in his study.[97]

We believe these geographical problems to have been far more static than scholars are usually prepared to accept. We do not, for example, see a necessity for changing the homeland of the Nine Bows from one period to another. We do not believe that the course of Egypt's history can ever have changed very dramatically in terms of population movements within Egypt itself, because it was an inland country and not easily open to any change. Nor do we believe that the situation in Retenu actually changed very much with the arrival of the Hurrite elements, who seem to have been largely absorbed.

What is vitally important is that we should reconstruct what facts we can *from the texts alone.* If we cannot make any sense of these, we cannot validly elucidate them from Aegean or Anatolian or any other sources. The texts must be allowed to speak for themselves and must be accepted *literally*, unless there are very good reasons for not doing so.

NOTES ON CHAPTER THREE

The following abbreviated references are used in this chapter:

Birch	S. Birch, "Mémoire sur une patère egyptienne du Musée du Louvre," *Mém. Soc. Imp. Ant. Fr.*, XXIV (1858).
Borchardt	L. Borchardt, *Das Grabdenkmal des Königs Sahure* (Leipzig, 1913).
Faulkner	R.O. Faulkner, *The Old Egyptian Pyramid Texts* (Oxford, 1969).
Gardiner I	A.H. Gardiner, *Ancient Egyptian Onomastica* (Oxford, 1947).
Gardiner II	A.H. Gardiner, *Late Egyptian Stories* (Bibliotheca Aegyptiaca, I, Brussels, 1932).

Griffith	F. Ll. Griffith, "The Abydos Decree of Seti I at Nauri," *JEA* XIII (1927).
Helck	W. Helck, *Der Einfluss der Militärführer in der 18. ägyptischen Dynastie* (Leipzig, 1939).
Iversen	E. Iversen, *Some Ancient Egyptian Paints and Pigments* (Copenhagen, 1955).
Kees	H. Kees, *Farbensymbolik in ägyptischen religiösen Texten* (Göttingen, 1943).
Kuentz	M.C. Kuentz, "Autour d'une conception égyptienne méconnue: l'*Akhit* ou soi-disant horizon," *BIFAO*, XVII.
Mercer	S.A.B. Mercer, *The Pyramid Texts* (London, 1952).
Montet	P. Montet, "Le nom des grecs en ancien égyptien," *Revue Archéologique*, XXVIII (1947).
Nibbi	A. Nibbi, *The Sea Peoples: A Re-examination of the Egyptian Sources* (Oxford, 1972).
Sethe	K. Sethe, *Die altägyptischen Pyramidentexte* (Glückstadt, 1908-22).
Thompson and Gaudet	K. Thompson and J. Gaudet, *A Review of Papyrus and its Role in Tropical Swamps* (1972) for *Archiv für Hydrobiologie*.
Vandersleyen	C. Vandersleyen, *Les guerres d'Amosis* (Brussels, 1971).
Vercoutter I	J. Vercoutter, "Les Haou-nebout," *BIFAO*, XLVI.
Vercoutter II	J. Vercoutter, "Les Haou-nebout," *BIFAO*, XLVIII.
Wilson	J.A. Wilson, trans., in J.B. Pritchard, ed., *Ancient Near Eastern Texts Relating to the Old Testament* (Princeton, 1969³).

1. J.F. Champollion, *Grammaire égyptienne* (Paris, 1836), p. 180.

2. Nibbi, chapter I.

3. A. Erman and H. Grapow, *Wörterbuch der ägyptischen Sprache*, 5 vols. (Leipzig, 1926-31), vol. I, p. 269; also H. Gauthier, *Dictionnaire des noms géographiques*, 7 vols. (Cairo, 1925-31), vol. I, pp. 41, 182; vol. II, p. 64; vol. IV, p. 190; vol. V, p. 1.

4. Sethe, pp. 628c, 1207a, 1213b, 1260b, 1505b, 1508c, 1925.

5. See Note 22, Chapter 2.

6. Faulkner, p. 171; Mercer, p. 179.

7. Faulkner, p. 144; Mercer, p. 150.

8. Nibbi, Preface.

9. Dr. Vandersleyen has collected all the examples of w3ḏ-wr that he could find, from all periods of Egyptian writing and hopes to establish a more exact meaning of the word, and of any changes in its meaning that have occurred.

10. Griffith, pp. 193ff.; see also Gardiner, *JEA*, XXXVIII (1952): 24ff.

11. Iversen, p. 6.

12. Iversen, p. 7.

13. Kees, pp. 435f.

14. Kees, p. 436.

15. Borchardt, Band II, Blatt 30.

16. F.W. Von Bissing, "La chambre des trois saisons du sanctuaire solaire du roi Rathoures," *Ann. Serv.* 53 (1956): p. 323 and plate V.

17. P. Lacau and H. Chévrier, *Une chapelle de Sesostris I* (Cairo, 1956), plate 27.

18. Oriental Institute, University of Chicago, *Medinet Habu*, 1964, plates 589 and 560.

19. E. Naville, *Deir-El-Bahari* (London, 1898), vol. V, plate CXXVIII.

20. W. Kelly Simpson, "Two Middle Kingdom Personifications of Seasons," *JNES*, XIII (1954): 265.

21. Also J. Leibovitch, "Gods of Agriculture and Welfare in Ancient Egypt," *JNES*, XII (1953): 73ff.

22. E.A. Wallis Budge, *Book of the Dead: The Papyrus of Ani* (British Museum, 1890), plate 8.

23. OnḤeḥ, see Gardiner, *Grammar*, Signlist C11; also *JEA*, XXVIII, plate IV; also Kees, *Götterglaube*, p. 312.

24. British Museum Hieratic Stela No. 138; F. Chabas, *Mélanges Egyptologiques* (1864), p. 335.

25. E. Suys, *La sagesse d'Ani* (Rome, 1935), p. 80.

26. Helck, pp. 22f.

27. Helck, p. 23.

28. Gardiner I, vol. I, p. 33*.

29. Gardiner I, vol. I, p. 113*.

30. K. Sethe, *Urk. IV*, p. 889.

31. Gardiner I, vol. I, p. 109*.

32. Gardiner, vol. I, pp. 33* and 34*.

33. Griffith, p. 199.

34. W.F. Edgerton and J.A.Wilson, *Historical Records of Ramesses III* (Chicago, 1936), p. 31, n. 53a.

35. These texts speak of the Nile or the inundation flowing into the Great Green, that is, of the Nile water losing itself in the rivulets and swampland of the Delta, where it physically disappeared.

36. Birch.

37. Birch, p. 19.

38. Gardiner II, pp. 61ff.; Wilson, pp. 25ff.

39. Gardiner II, pp. 76ff.; Wilson, trans., pp. 17f.

40. Gardiner I, I, p. 162*f.

41. *Medinet Habu*, plate 600; see frontispiece.

42. Papyrus Harris, Historical section.

43. K.A. Kitchen, *Ramesside Inscriptions* IV, 2, pp. 2f.; J. Breasted, *Ancient Records of Egypt* (Chicago, 1906), vol. III, par. 572ff. See also Chapter Four.

44. J.A. Knudtzon, *Die El Amarna Tafeln* (Leipzig, 1908) and S.A.B. Mercer, *The Tell el-Amarna Tablets* (Toronto, 1939), Letters 101, 105, 129, 132.

45. The Wadi Tumilat has been discussed in Chapter Two, and will be referred to again in Chapter Six, on shipping.

46. This has already been discussed in Chapter Two.

47. Gardiner I, I, pp. 194*f.

48. H. Brugsch, *Dictionnaire géographique* (1879), p. 180.

49. A. Nibbi, "Further Remarks on w3ḏ-wr, Sea Peoples and Keftiu," *Göttinger Miszellen,* 10 (1974).

50. A.H. Gardiner, *Egyptian Grammar,* (London, 1957³), see 'sandy tract' sign, N. 18, 'earth or land' sign, N. 16, 'circuit' sign, Z 8, and the 'loaf', X 5.

51. M.C. Kuentz, "Autour d'une conception égyptienne méconnue: l'*Akhit* ou soi-disant horizon," *BIFAO,* XVII, pp. 148ff.

52. Vercoutter II, pp. 111ff.

53. Kuentz, p. 152.

54. Kuentz, p. 156.

55. Gardiner I, I, pp. 207*f.

56. J.E. Quibell, *Hierakonpolis* (London, 1900), plates XXV and XXVIc.

57. W.M. Flinders Petrie, *Ceremonial Slate Palettes* (London, 1953), p. 14 and plates D and E.

58. Reference as for Note 22, plate 35.

59. A.H. Gardiner, *The Wilbour Papyrus,* II, Commentary (Oxford, 1948), pp. 26f.

60. Vercoutter I, pp. 125ff. and II, pp. 107ff.

61. C. Vandersleyen, *Les guerres d'Amosis* (Brussels, 1971), pp. 139ff.

62. E. Uphill, "The Nine Bows," *JEOL* (1967): 193ff.

63. P. Montet, "Le nom des grecs en ancien égyptien," *Revue Archéologique,* XXVIII (1947): 129ff.; ibid., XXXIV (1946): 129ff.; ibid., XXXII (1956), 1ff.

64. Vercoutter I, pp. 132f.

65. Vercoutter I, p. 138.

66. Vercoutter I, p. 144; see also Gardiner I, I, pp. 206*ff.

67. Gardiner I, I, p. 207*.

68. See Note 24, Chapter 2.

69. Thompson and Gaudet, section I.

70. Thompson and Gaudet, p. 12.

71. Vercoutter I, p. 147, taken from De Buck, *Coffin Texts,* II, 160b-c.

72. Vercoutter II, p. 144, taken from Chassinat-Palanque, "Une campagne de Fouilles dans la nécropole d'Assiout,"Mém. *IFAOC, XXIV,* 108, var. 212.

73. Sethe, vol. I, pp. 339f.; also Faulkner, p. 120; Mercer, p. 125, n.6.

74. Sethe, vol. I, pp. 471f.; Faulkner, p. 151; Mercer, p. 157.

75. Sethe, vol. II, pp. 362f.; Faulkner, p. 244; Mercer, pp. 250f.

76. Vercoutter I, pp. 146f.

77. Vercoutter I, pp. 147.

78. P. Montet, pp. 2ff.

79. Borchardt, Band II, Blatt 19.

80. Vercoutter II, p. 149.

81. A. Sneh and T. Weissbrod, "Nile Delta: The Defunct Pelusiac Branch Identified," *Science,* Vol. 180 (April, 1973): pp. 59ff.

82. Vercoutter II, p. 183.

83. A. Erman and V. Wilcken, "Die Naucratis Stele," *ZAS,* XXXVIII (1900): 127ff.; also Gunn, *JEA,* 29 (1943): 58.

84. Vercoutter II, pp. 176f.; also Vandersleyen, pp. 144f.

85. Montet, pp. 2ff.

86. Vandersleyen, pp. 102ff.

87. G.A. Reisner and M.B. Reisner, "Inscribed Monuments from Gebel Barkal," *ZAS,* LXIX, pp. 29f., line 14.

88. Vercoutter II, p. 121.

89. Vercoutter II, p. 122; see also Alan Gardiner's study of ḥnwt, *JEA,* 29 (1943): 38, n. 2.

90. Vercoutter II, p. 125.

91. A. Scharff, "Der Historische Abschnitt der Lehre für König Merikarê," *SBAW* (1936), Heft 8; Gardiner, trans., *JEA,* I (1914): 20ff., also Wilson, pp. 414ff.

92. Gardiner I, I, pp. 171*f.

93. N. de Garis Davies, *Tombs of Two Officials,* plate XXVIII.

94. Wörterbuch, II, 286. 11.

95. Gardiner I, I, p. 172*.

96. Gardiner I, I, pp. 171ff*.

97. W. Helck, *Beziehungen,* pp. 277f.

The Contents of the Texts

The Attacks in the Time of Ramesses III*

Reports of the attacks on the Egyptian frontier by foreigners during the reign of Ramesses III come from the inscriptions on the walls of his Mortuary Temple at Medinet Habu and from a few lines in the long and well-preserved Papyrus Harris, completed at about the time of his death.

The records at Medinet Habu have a bombastic style which has unfortunately caused many scholars to treat them with mistrust so that their contents have not received sufficient attention either linguistically or as historical records. Even if they are long-winded in their praise for the Pharaoh or in their descriptions of the humiliation of the enemy, invariably defeated, these inscriptions make some explicit statements about events at this time which we cannot disregard. There is undoubtedly some repetition in these texts from records of earlier periods and certain linguistic difficulties make for many uncertainties, but a number of statements they contain ought to be considered seriously.

It is also important to see the documents in their proper historical setting, which includes taking into account Egypt's

*All the translated extracts used in this section are taken from W.F. Edgerton and J.A. Wilson: *Historical Records of Ramesses III*, Oriental Institute, University of Chicago, 1936.

relationship with the peoples in the countries nearby, as reflected in all the documents available to us from this period and not merely to see the attacks on her frontiers as isolated events, unrelated to anything else that was happening at the time. Nor should we ignore the previous attacks on Egypt's frontiers which are to be found in the records, not only from the reign of Merenptah, but in the reigns of several other pharaohs as well.

Scholars of Greek and Anatolian history have attached great importance to one passage from the inscription of year 8, always quoted to explain the destruction wrought in the Aegean and the Hittite lands at the end of the Bronze Age. It begins: "As for the foreign countries, they made a conspiracy in their isles. . . . " (It will be quoted in full below.) Scholars have repeatedly taken these few lines in isolation, to prove an invasion of unknown warriors from an unknown north. But nothing could be more misleading. Apart from the fact that the translation of these passages presents many difficulties and that the rendering of 'conspiracy' and 'isles' leaves room for a great deal of discussion on the part of Egyptologists, the whole of the inscription must be read and the passage seen in its original context if the truth is to be arrived at.

The facts presented by the inscription of year 8 are remarkably simple and straightforward when the bombast and the linguistic difficulties are set aside. It says in its introduction:

> Year 8 under the majesty of Horus. . . . Mighty Bull, strong lion, mighty of arm, possessor of a strong arm, taking captive the Asiatics (Sttyw, with a determinative for both men and women) . . . destroying the Nine Bows driven from their land . . . the King . . . causing the Asiatics to turn back (by) fighting on the (battlefield). As for the rebels (who know not) Egypt forever, they hear of his strength coming with praise . . . they say to their people: "His form and his body are exactly equal to those of Baal."[1]

The Egyptians are recording events which took place in the eighth year of the reign of Ramesses III and they say that they have taken captive the Asiatics, people from areas to the north of Egypt who had rebelled against her. The Egyptians have defeated the enemy and driven them out of their lands. We are speaking here of the lands of the enemy. The conquered people are shown in the reliefs as was customary, praising the Pharaoh after their defeat and saying that he was the very image of Baal.

The name of this god is written in full as was usual with all the foreign gods. We know that Baal was worshipped throughout the Canaanite lands and became well-known in Egypt after this country's conquests in the north, more particularly during the nineteenth and twentieth dynasties, when Baal came to be equated with Seth. In another part of the Great (Mortuary) Temple at Medinet Habu we find reliefs showing prisoners labelled respectively Peleset, Denyen and Shekelesh, making a similar reference to Baal.[2] We shall return to this point later.

After the introduction quoted above, this same text goes on to praise the Pharaoh at some length and then to the often quoted passage:

> As for the foreign countries, they made a (conspiracy) in their isles (rww). (Removed) and scattered in the fray were the lands at one time. No land could stand before their arms, from Hatti, Kode, Carchemish, Yereth and Yeres on, (but they were) cut off at (one time). A camp (was set up) in one place in Amor. They desolated its people, and its land was like that which has never come into being. They were coming, while the flame was prepared before them, forward toward Egypt. Their confederation was the Peleset, Theker, Denye(n) and the Weshesh, lands united. They laid their hands upon the lands to the (very) circuit of the earth, their hearts confident and trusting: "Our plans will succeed."[3]

With regard to terminology, it is necessary to recall here that the foreign countries in these texts are written ḫ3swt 'hill-countries' and that not all the names of foreign countries set out in the inscriptions carry the hill-country determinative even where there is room for it. This term must be linked, literally as it suggests, with 'hill-countries' as opposed to 'plains'. Having said this, however, we must not exclude the possibility that, the Egyptians being such traditionalists, they might not continue to apply the name of 'hill-countries' to those Asiatics who had later settled in the area of the eastern Delta and the Bitter Lakes. In the story of Sinhue this term is used exclusively for the western Asiatic city states, as it is in many other texts later. We referred in an earlier chapter to the common use in Egyptian of 'isles' (ỉww and rww) for inland areas and for Asiatic settlements.

Much has been made of the statement: "No land could stand before them," but this was a standard expression found elsewhere in the Egyptian texts, for example, in a text of Hor-em-heb: "no land could stand before him."[4] It does not have any special significance here, except to exaggerate the strength of the enemy so that the Egyptian victory might be seen as all the greater.

This passage of the inscription refers to a geographically far-reaching area of destruction wrought by Egypt's attackers, from the Hittite lands all the way down to the borders of Egypt. Nothing is said about the duration of time of these attacks, but they must have been slow-moving. The pictorial record shows Egypt's attackers to have come south with heavy ox-carts, accompanied by women and children. This is hardly the equipment for a lightning war, nor the way in which an attacking army would move in foreign territory, with enemies in every direction including the rear. There was also the physical obstacle of what one Egyptian document calls ". . . the impenetrable hill-countries of the Fenkhu."[5]

Dr. Barnett's statement[6] that the draft oxen shown in the reliefs were not used in the Aegean or in Palestine is difficult to support if we remember that these humped oxen are shown in the Egyptian monuments of the eighteenth dynasty, as Helck has pointed out.[7] A scene in the tomb of Kenamun (Tomb 162, Thebes) showed unmistakable Syrians bringing tribute to Egypt and among their gifts are humped cattle.[8] The tomb dates probably from the time of Amenophis III. The picture also carries a detail that could be taken as an example of a child being presented to Egypt by his mother as tribute. The women present in this scene wear the flounced dress that we have come to associate with Crete.

It is therefore clear that humped cattle were known and used in Egypt at this time, and also in Syria. The Canaanite lands are constantly mentioned in the Egyptian documents as providers of cattle for Egypt.

Bearing in mind the extent of the area threatened and destroyed by the enemy it seems reasonable to conclude that the only people who would have been in a position freely to attack both the Hittite states and the Egyptian frontier, travelling by ox-carts with solid wooden wheels over "impenetrable hill-country" would be the people who were actually at home in the area between the two. Only "local" people could hope to reach either frontier without being decimated first. One cannot imagine outsiders attempting to do this in similar conditions, and accompanied by women and children.

Our text says that a camp was set up in Amor or Amurru in northern Syria. Egypt's attackers therefore appear to have had a far more comfortable central rallying point in this region than any migrating group or foreign army could possibly be expected to have.

Amurru appears to have been the traditionally important centre for Syrian rebels against Egypt. In the Amarna period, it had been the centre of activity for the rebel leaders of these states, Abdi-Ashirta and his sons. The seizure of Amurru by Egypt's attackers in year 8 of the reign of Ramesses III may well have been the climax of their rebellion, a symbolical gesture for the rebel cause, the "conspiracy" of the text, because the earlier inscription of year 5 mentions the defeat and capture of Amurru by Egypt. The explicit mention of the capture of this state by each side in turn emphasizes the importance of this region in relation to the hostilities.

Dr. Kupper in his study of Amurru and the Amorites has shown that we have still much to learn about this area and the people in it throughout the centuries.[9] In a more recent study, Dr. Koenig has discussed the interesting problem of Amurru's assimilation of Israel.[10] But most important of all, we find that the most positive statement that can be made for this area is the result of Dr. Van Seter's researches,[11] namely that the Hyksos rulers of Egypt included Amorites, as well as the other groups of Asiatics, mentioned traditionally in the Egyptian texts. Dr. Koenig believes that these peoples formed a federation in the first half of the second millennium, this being confirmed by the execration texts studied by Sethe and Posener.[12]

Gardiner pointed out that the first mention of Amurru that we have in the Egyptian texts, apart from the cuneiform Amarna letters, is from the time of Sethos I.[13] An Egyptian text from Karnak tells us that Sethos I went northwards to destroy the land of Kadesh and the land of Amurru. This state is also mentioned twice in the Kadesh texts of Ramesses II. We may remember that a prince of Amurru is portrayed in our labelled list of northern prisoners from Medinet Habu, reproduced as our frontispiece.[14]

The names of Egypt's attackers as they appear in the texts have always been a problem, and they have been variously identified, inconclusively, except for the Peleset.[15] Scholars seem to agree that these are the Philistines and there appears to be nothing to contradict this. Otherwise many difficulties remain such as the time of their arrival in western Asia and the nature of their culture.

However, one cannot sufficiently stress, even to Egyptologists, that most of the names on the many Egyptian lists of enemies cannot be identified, and the recognition of Aegean names in the Egyptian texts should be seen for what it is, namely an interesting, speculative exercize.

Returning to our text of year 8, we note the use of the expression "the circuit of the earth." Obviously this is to be understood as relating to Egypt's concept of the extent of the earth, and not ours. We have already said that the Delta was not a two-way system of communication with the world overseas, as far as Egypt was concerned. It served rather to cut her off from the world. The chapter on shipping which follows emphasizes that there is not a shred of evidence, textual or otherwise, to show that the Egyptians ever went to sea in pharaonic times. The assumption of an active Egyptian trade with the world beyond the Near East is not supported by much documentary evidence. Expressions such as "the Great Circle" and "the circuit of the earth" have to be understood, as we have already said, from within the geographically limited Egyptian way of life, no easy task for us. We should begin by assuming they have a physical basis. In the same way, as far back as the fifth dynasty, we find expressions like "smiter of all countries" meaning clearly only those countries within the reach of Egypt's armies at that time.

Immediately following upon the passage we quoted last from the inscription of year 8, naming the Peleset, Tjekker, Shekelesh, Denyen and Weshesh, we find a description of the battle given by the Pharaoh, which has largely been neglected and which ought to be looked at in its entirety for the value of its detail. Very important is the statement at the beginning of the quotation where the Pharaoh says that his way of dealing with the attackers was to organize his frontier in Djahy. The text suggests that only one area is being prepared to counter the expected attack by water and by land.

> I organized my frontier in Zahi (Djahy) prepared before them (to wit) the princes, the commanders of the garrisons and the Mariannu. I caused the Nile mouth to be prepared like a strong wall with war-ships, galleys and coasters, (equipped), for they were manned completely from bow to stern with valiant warriors with their weapons; the militia

consisting of every picked man of Egypt were like lions roaring up the mountains tops. The chariotry consisted of runners, of (picked men), of every good and capable chariot warrior. Their horses were quivering in every part of their bodies, ready to crush the countries (hill-countries) under their hoofs. I was a valiant Montu, standing fast at their head. . . . As for those who reached my frontier, their seed is not, their heart and their soul are finished for ever. As for those who came forward together on the (Great Green), the full flame was in front of them at the Nile mouths, while a stockade of lances surrounded them on the (canal)[16] (so that they were) dragged (to land),[17] hemmed in, prostrated on the (bank), slain and made into heaps, heels over head. Their ships and their goods were as if fallen into the water . . . since I have sat on the throne of Harakhte . . . I have not let the (hill-) countries behold the frontier of Egypt, to boast thereof to the Nine Bows. I have taken away their land, their frontiers being added to mine. Their chiefs and their tribespeople are mine with praise . . . the gods made me to be King in Egypt, to strengthen her, to repel for her the plains and hill-countries . . . no land has stood firm at the sound of thy name, but they leave their settlements, (moving away) from their place . . . weeping is in the countries and trembling in every land. . . . [18]

It seems from this text that the Pharaoh's frontier in Djahy is at the northernmost point of the Nile before its waters separated into the various streams of the Delta. We have already referred to various texts which suggest that Retenu or Djahy began in the eastern Delta.[19] It was at this point that the Pharaoh marshalled his river forces, carrying his militia, and set out his chariotry in readiness. It seems that some of the enemy descended towards the Nile proper from further north in the Delta (the Great Green) and these were met with a wall of fire which the Egyptians had prepared for them. That part of the enemy that came along the canal (mr, line 24) are those which are shown in the so-called Sea Battle, and slaughtered by the Pharaoh's waiting archers.

The Pharaoh's boast that he has not allowed the hill-countries to look upon the frontier of Egypt means that while Ramesses III was King, he was able to repel the enemy before they reached the Nile proper, or the area around Heliopolis. The settlements he is referring to here are more likely to be those Asiatic settlements we have already referred to in the Delta[20] than those further north in Palestine and Syria. The expressions "I have taken away their lands, I have added their frontiers to mine" are not stock expressions in the Egyptian idiom, and are probably meant to be taken quite literally. This is a further reason for thinking that the area referred to here is the eastern Delta.

The implication in this text is that the hill-countries had been trying to enter Egypt for some time while the watchful eye of the Pharaoh had prevented them from doing so. The enemy's lands had been taken away, a thing which the Pharaoh could not have done had the lands been further afield. Nor could he have added their lands to his own if they had not been immediately adjoining the frontiers of Egypt. Since he says he has driven them from their settlements and towns, they could not have been nomadic peoples, nor could they have been tribes in transit, from Asia Minor or elsewhere. It is quite clear from the text that he has defeated these peoples on their own lands, and he calls the enemy "the hill-countries."

In this same text the Pharaoh goes on to say:

> (As for the) foreign (countries) . . . ˙destruction to their towns, devastated at one time; their trees and all their people are become ashes. They take counsel with their hearts: "Whither shall we go?" (Their chiefs) come . . . (their children and their tribute upon) their backs, to Egypt. . . .[21]

The reference to the destruction of the trees is an interesting one, because this was normal practice in the Egyptian treatment of a defeated Asiatic town. Egypt attached great importance to trees because of the scarcity of wood in Egypt. Asiatic territory was renowned for its timber and not only in the area which we know as the Lebanon today. In his study of the woodlands of ancient western Asia, Dr. M. B. Rowton concluded that the hill-country of Syria and Palestine had very much more woodland in the second millennium than it has today.[22] He believes that the coastal range which extends southwards from the mouth of the Orontes into Upper Galilee, small though it is, retained very substantial forest right down to the Hellenistic period, in spite of urban settlement. Even after this period he believed deforestation to be a very slow process.[23]

The Bitter Lakes area and the eastern Delta, being well provided with water, must have included trees among the vegetation, though they may not have been pines of the finest category.

There are a number of recorded instances of the cutting down of trees by the victorious Egyptians, and all follow the defeat of an Asiatic town. The monuments of Tuthmosis III tell us that his men had cut down the trees after the defeat of Kadesh, Ardata and the towns of Naharin.[24] Similarly, Ramesses III's defeat of Tunip is recorded by showing soldiers cutting down its trees[25] (Plate XII). The value which the Egyptians of that time set upon these trees is recorded on the Barkal Stela:

> Every year there is hewn for me in Djahy genuine cedar of Lebanon which is brought to the Court . . . each and every year. . . . When my army which is in the garrison of Ullaza comes (they) bring tribute which is the cedar of the victories of my majesty, through the plans of my father, (Amon-Re) who entrusted to me all foreign countries. I have not given (any) of it to the Asiatics (for) it is a wood which he loves.
> . . .[26]

This suggests a possible monopoly of ship-building timber by Egypt.

Among the concluding lines of the inscription of year 8 we find the Pharaoh styled "Ruler of the Nine Bows." This means that Egypt claimed sovereignty over these traditional enemies, whom she termed rebels.

The Inscription of Year 5[27]

This is an earlier inscription than the one we have already spoken of and it refers principally to the activities of the Libyans. However, passages from this have also been generally quoted by historians with reference to the attackers of Egypt's frontier. Because of the similarity of certain passages in this text with those of the inscription of year 8, scholars have wondered whether the scribes were not embellishing the later records by repeating some of the colourful passages from earlier ones. This is possible. It is also possible that the cutting of this inscription was delayed for several years, as was sometimes the case, so that, because of its mixed content, this particular record is considered not to be reliable in dating the attack by the northern countries on Egypt's frontier.

Nevertheless, a careful look at the text of year 5 shows the circumstances of the fighting to be different from those of year 8.

It begins with the usual abundant praise for the valour, skill and importance of the Pharaoh who has led his victorious armies against the Tehenu or Libyans, a general term to include all western enemies. These are called the "arrogant" countries in line 13. Egypt has defeated the chief of Amurru and his army and the survivors come to do homage to the Pharaoh. Hence the need, three years later, as we have already said, for the attackers of Egypt to win back Amurru.

The text goes on to tell us:

> The plains and hill-countries were cut off and carried away to Egypt as slaves, presented all together to its Ennead. Satisfaction, food and supplies abound in the Two Lands. The multitude rejoices in this land and there is no sorrow, for Amon-Re has established his son in his place, so that all that the sun-disc encircles is united in his grasp. The Asiatic and Libyan enemies are carried off who were (formerly) ruling Egypt, so that the land lay desolate in complete destruction since kings (began) while they persecuted the gods as well as everybody, and there was no hero to (receive them when they rebelled). . . .[28]

This is followed by more praise for the Pharaoh and his soldiers: "his name and the terror of him burn up the plains and hill-countries."[29]

As the story unfolds, not too clearly at this point, we find that there was trouble about the succession to a Libyan chieftainship:

> The land of Temeh was come, gathered together in one place, consisting of Rebu, Seped and Meshwesh. . . . Their warriors relied on their plans, coming, their hearts confident: "We will (advance) ourselves!" Their plans in their bodies were: "We will act." (Their) hearts were full of wrongdoing with perversity but their plan was shattered and turned aside. . . . They asked a chief with their mouth. . . . His majesty had brought a little one of the land of Temeh, a child, (supported) by his strong arms, appointed for them to be a chief, to regulate their land. . . .[30]

The inscription tells us that these rebels suffered a crushing defeat on their own soil after attacking Egypt's frontier.

> They were made into pyramids on their (own) soil. . . . Every survivor was brought captive to Egypt. . . . The chiefs of the foreign countries were assembled, beholding their misery. . . . The backbone of Temeh is broken for the duration of eternity . . . their feet (have ceased) to tread the frontier of Egypt. . . .[31]

There follows an extended declaration of the might of Egypt and the abject state of the defeated peoples. Straight after this, without any linking passage, we have the following, well-known lines which the document treats as the logical continuation of what goes before.

> The northern countries quivered in their bodies, namely the Peleset, Thekk(er). . . . They were cut off (from) their land, coming, their spirit broken. They were thr-warriors on land; another (group) was on the (Great Green). . . . [32]

This certainly appears to be an attack by water similar to the one recorded later and more fully in the inscription of year 8. If we were to accept this as a record of the events of year 5, and quite separate from those of year 8, then we should have to account for two attacks on Egypt by water-borne foreigners, in the Delta, within a few years of each other. This is not impossible. We must not exclude the possibility of repeated attacks of this kind in actual fact. The Egyptian records are full of references to continuous skirmishing and fighting with Asiatic groups adjoining her territories. We must not exclude the possibility that this included the use of canals leading into the Bitter Lakes area and along the eastern Delta generally. It is to be hoped that we may learn more about these canals in the not too distant future. The record of year 8 clearly tells us that the fighting against Egypt's attackers took place near the Nile proper, somewhere in the vicinity of Heliopolis, and not further afield. In addition to this, we must remember how prominently these problems are featured in the records of the reign of Ramesses III. So it is not to be excluded that the attacks by the Asiatic groups in the north were continuous and frequent.

Immediately after this passage, we have a warning to those "who plot in their hearts against Egypt," because no country can withstand the strength of Egypt's Pharaoh.[33]

The document concludes with a description of the peace which prevails in the country after the Pharaoh's victories:

> The land is like a slab; for there is no greed and a woman may go according to her wish, with her clothing on her head, her step unhindered, to the place which she desires. The foreign countries come bowing to the glory of his majesty, with their tribute and their children upon their backs. The southerners like the northerners are his in praise. . . . [34]

There is no reference here to any special characteristic of the attackers from the north. It is, in fact, clearly implied in the text that there is no more drama attached to their attack than to the hostilities of the people from the south. The historical section of the Papyrus Harris also contains a passage reminiscent of this one.

No one could call this a rambling and disjointed document. It has a definite literary style and a closely-knit pattern for telling its story. Its seventy-five lines are divided up into sections, of differing lengths, it is true, but each one a unit concluding with a variety of flattering epithets for the Pharaoh and his name. It is coherent as it stands.

We would tend to the view that it is an authentic document on the grounds that some of the Asiatic groups attacking Egypt were clearly sedentary populations in the eastern Delta and the area of the Bitter Lakes. That there should be fighting between them and Egypt is to be expected. Moreover, the fate of Amurru in the two documents is not the same. In the inscription of year 5 it is Egypt who is victorious while in the later document of year 8, Amurru is won back by the rebels. This is one of the very few admissions of inadequacy by Egypt in any of her documents.

Other Inscriptions from the Time of Ramesses III

We cannot really separate the Libyans from the other attackers of Egypt. The documents show them to be very closely related in their interests.

An inscription on the exterior west wall of the Mortuary Temple at Medinet Habu says:

> Then came one to say to his Majesty: "The Tehenu are in motion; they are making a conspiracy. They are gathered and assembled without number, consisting of Rebu, Seped and Meshwesh, lands assembled to advance themselves against Egypt."[35]

On this occasion, it is the Tehenu who are conspiring against Egypt. This is a cumulative term for all the western enemies of Egypt and more particularly all the Libyan tribes. We are told here that they have transgressed Egypt's frontiers and their motive is stated to be a desire for more power, or perhaps, independence from Egyptian rule. It is difficult to imagine that this could possibly mean that the Libyan tribes intended to take

Egypt over completely. In an inscription in the interior of the Temple, we find these words over the King:

> My arm has overthrown the Tehenu, who came prepared, their hearts confident, to lift themselves up in rivalry with Egypt.[36]

On the exterior west wall of the Temple we see a general reference to Egypt's enemies, in words spoken by Mont:

> Thy father Amon has sent thee forth, that he may cast down for thee the rebellious ones . . . mayest thou go out in strength and return in valour against every land that attacks thee.[37]

Clearly then, both Libyans and others were considered at this time to be rebels against Egyptian rule rather than armies wanting to take over Egypt, even though the Libyans are said on two occasions elsewhere to have wanted to settle in Egypt.

In another text from the exterior north wall of the Temple, we find the Libyan tribes mentioned together with Peleset and the Asiatics in general. We see Ramesses III issuing fighting equipment to his troops for a campaign in which Sherden and Nubians are fighting on the Egyptian side: Over the officials we find:

> Thou art Re . . . . Great is thy strength in the heart of the Nine (Bows) . . . . The heart of the land of Temeh is removed, the Peleset (are in suspense hidden in their towns . . . . [Before the King:] . . . Bring forth equipment! Send out troops to destroy the rebellious (countries) which know not Egypt . . . [On a horizontal line in the centre of the scene:] Usermare Meriamon, the mighty bull, crushing the Asiatics, lord of . . . in the lands . . . entering (into) the midst . . . . [Over two scribes in the centre:] . . . giving . . . equipment to the infantry and chariotry, to the troops, the Sherden and the Nubians. [Over the officials at the base:] Our lord goes forth in valour, so that he may plunder the plains and hill countries . . . .[38]

Here the Peleset are clearly spoken of as being hidden (?) in their towns, presumably with the Egyptian armies looking for them. Unless this scene is to be dismissed as absolute nonsense, we cannot dissociate the references to the Peleset, the rebellious countries, the Asiatics and the plains and hill-countries placed in such proximity as they are here. It is also clear from this text that the Pharaoh and his troops were going out into enemy territory to plunder the towns. There is no mention of water travel or of boats here.

We know that the land of Syria and Palestine had always been for Egypt a source of great wealth in terms of valuable materials which were either plundered or extorted as tribute. We cannot therefore be surprised to read of rebellion in these lands against their Egyptian oppressors, nor of Egypt's determination to keep them in subjection.

Still on the same wall of the Temple, we are shown the King marching towards Djahy accompanied by Egyptian and foreign troops, a scene very similar to another on the same wall, but containing less detail. Before the King:

> The King, rich in strength as he goes forth abroad, great of fear and awe in the heart of the Asiatics. [Behind the King:] His majesty sets out in valour and strength to destroy the rebellious countries. [Over the troops at the base:] His majesty sets out for Djahy like unto Montu, to crush every country that violates his frontier. . . . King of Upper and Lower Egypt, Ruler of the Nine Bows, Lord of the Two Lands. . . . [39]

The identity of the people attacking Egypt could hardly be more clearly stated. Here the Asiatics are referred to as rebels and we are told that the Pharaoh is setting out to go abroad to the Canaanite lands (Djahy) to punish those who have attacked the Egyptian frontier. We have to accept the facts as they are stated, and cannot dismiss as nonsense a record on the major Temple of the area. Moreover, it is important to note that the text expressly states that the Pharaoh claimed to be ruler of these enemies. The only other people ever recorded as having been punished for transgressing Egypt's frontier are the Libyans, in the extract we quoted earlier.

What is actually being described in these texts is continual border fighting and skirmishing in the Delta area.

Immediately following upon the scene we have described above we see the Pharaoh in battle with the land forces of the enemy.[40] This scene shows Ramesses III charging into an enemy which is portrayed as helpless. Some of the enemy are on foot, while others are in ox-carts, including their women and children. This scene is often quoted as proof that the enemy were coming to settle in Egypt, but in fact, before the King, we have the words: " . . . trampling down the plains and hill-countries (which are) prostrate, beaten from tail to head before his horses.''[41] The inscription is unfortunately very brief here, but the enemy is clearly called "the plains and hill-countries" which is a common term for the western Asiatic peoples in the Egyptian records. No mention is ever made that this particular group of attackers were coming to settle in Egypt, or that it was ever their intention.

The well-known picture showing the Egyptian fleet in battle with enemy ships[42] cannot be discussed without some reference to the way in which it is portrayed on the exterior north wall of the Temple. These reliefs are now very difficult to see, not only because they are high up on the wall of the Temple, but also because they have lost all their colour and much of their surface, the relief having now worn quite thin. However, we are fortunate in having the Medinet Habu reproductions published by the Oriental Institute of the University of Chicago. Four Egyptian boats are shown defeating five enemy ones with some prowess, because the enemy ships are surrounded and forced towards land, where some Egyptian archers are waiting for them. The enemy is in confusion and in the lower register we see a long row of prisoners being led off. The text tells us that the attack came from a channel (mr) inside the Great Green. There is no evidence whatever that it took place on the open sea, and this is in fact contrary to what the text actually says. In the scene of this battle some lines of text before the King say: "The good god, Montu in Egypt, great of strength like Baal in the foreign countries, strong of arms, undaunted of heart, haughty, skilled in his strength, a great wall for sheltering Egypt, so that there may come no land to injure it. . . . ''[43]

It is no accident that at this point which is a climax in Egypt's recorded victory against the enemy, Baal, the god of the Asiatics, is again invoked. The Egyptian god Mont is stated to be as powerful as Baal was in the northern hill-countries.

Following the passage quoted above we find, behind the King: "Now the northern (hill-countries) which were in their isles were quivering in their bodies. They penetrated the channels of the Nile mouths. . . . Their weapons are scattered in the (Great Green).''[44]

Still on the same wall we find Ramesses III standing on a rostrum before a fortress while his officials are presenting to him as captives the same people as those we saw in the "Sea Battle."

Scribes are recording the numbers of two piles of severed hands while two rows of captives are led to Egyptian officials. In this scene the text before the King reads:

> . . . as for the foreign (hill-countries) who came from their land in the isles in the midst of the . . . (Great Green) . . . as they were (coming) forward toward Egypt, their heart relying upon their hands, a net was prepared before them, to ensnare them. They that entered the Nile Mouths were (caught), fallen into the midst of it. . . . Amon-Re repels my foe and gives to me every land (t3) into my grasp. [Over the officials:] . . . Thou art Re. . . . Thy strength crushes the Nine Bows and every land (t3) trembles at thy name. [Before a prince:] Amon is the god who decreed the protection to the ruler of every land (t3). [Before the span:] Live the good god . . . making every foreign (hill-) country (ḥswt) non-existent. . . .[45]

In our chapter on the Great Green, we have already said that *the middle islands* (islands in the midst) were islands in the Nile streams, and in the chapter on the Delta, we stressed the Asiatic settlements there, which we believe the Egyptians to have continued to call ḥswt because of their origins and allegiances in this respect.

It is very likely that "the net" mentioned in this text is a physical one, of the large kinds we see in the Egyptian tomb paintings for catching fish. It sounds here as though a net was thrown across the canal along which the enemy was expected, in order to stop them from proceeding any further. The system of catching the enemy on the river by a net is referred to by W. Wolf in his comments on a hymn to Ptah.[46] The text leaves us in no doubt that the Egyptians knew where to lie in wait for the enemy, so it is quite likely that the enemy had no choice about the way it approached the Egyptians.

One scene on the same wall shows Ramesses III presenting captives from the "Sea Battle" and Libyans, together, to the Theban Triad who are in a shrine. The inscription over Amon says:

> . . . Welcome in joy! For thou hast slain the Nine Bows and hast overthrown everyone who assailed thee. Thou hast cast down the hearts of the Asiatics, for thou hast taken away the breath from their nostrils . . . . [Before the King:] I went forth that I might plunder the Nine Bows and slay all lands. Not a land stood firm before me, but I cut off their root. I have re-

turned in valour my arms (laden) with captives, the leaders of every land . . . .[47]

The captives shown in this scene are in two registers. Above we have people in Sherden-type kilts and corselets but with feathered headdresses. There are no Sherden-type helmets worn by this group. On the lower register there are bearded men in long tunics with the typical Libyan side-curl. Right at the bottom of this scene, in a horizontal line, we have one of those rows of bound, bearded prisoners, each representing a group or tribe of people whose name is written inside a name-ring. This inscription is damaged but we are able to see fourteen captives, seven of which have the hill-country determinative with their names. They are: Naharin, Tunip, Pebekh, Katna, Isi, Segerkh and Yerteg. The others do not have this determinative. They are: the ḥ3w nbwt, Tenep, Lower Egypt, Menesen, the people of the western oases, the people of the eastern desert and the Tehenu.[48]

Over these prisoners we find the words: "All lands, the Fenkhu, the circuit of the heavens, all mankind, all people, all the ḥ3w nbwt, all folk are under the feet of this good god whom all the people praise. . . . [49]

We have to accept these as the countries from which the hostilities spoken of in these texts emanated. These lands, together with Nubia, were the areas from which Egypt expected trouble at this particular time. We do not recognise all the countries or cities mentioned on this list[50] but we see that many of them are Egypt's traditional enemies from the past records.

In this same scene, there is a most important inscription over the captives in feathered headdresses: "Words spoken by the great fallen ones of the Thekker who are in the grasp of his majesty. . . . Great is thy strength, O mighty King, Great Sun of Egypt! Greater is thy sword than a mountain of metal, while the awe of thee is like (that of) Baal. . . . [51] This is an unusual line of praise for the Pharaoh used again elsewhere by people shown to be wearing exactly the same dress and called in the text: the Peleset, Denyen and Shekelesh.[52] The reference to Baal by these people is significant and needs no further comment at this point, although the name of Baal is in this case written by the determinative only (as for Seth). The reference to the mountain of metal (b3) is most interesting and can indicate a number of possibilities for rebellion by the near eastern states. A similar reference is to be found in the earlier "Israel" Stela from the time of Merenptah, where the mountain of metal is said to have been "on the neck of the people" during the evil times which were formerly over Egypt during which the temples of Memphis had been neglected.[53] The reference here seems to be to the Asiatic rule in Egypt which ignored the local gods. In the Ramesside context the expression "mountain of metal" appears to be equated with the Asiatics.

A scene similar to the one we have just referred to is found in the interior of the Temple where the Pharaoh is presenting captives to Amon and Mut, while a sickle sword is being offered to the King.[54] The captives are all in Sherden-type kilts and corselets but wear feathered headdresses. Here the text clearly calls the captives "Asiatics" ('3mw), the determinative showing both men and women, in line 3, while their groups are named as Peleset, Denyen and Shekelesh, although no distinction is made in their dress.[55] The document says, before Amon:

> . . . Thou hast taken captive him who assailed thee and hast slain him who violated thy frontier. My sword was with thee, overthrowing for thee the lands. Thou hast cut off the heads of the Asiatics . . . . [Before the King:] . . . . Thy sword is mine as a shield, that I may slay the plains and hill-countries which violate my frontier. Thou causest the awe of me to be great in the hearts of their chiefs . . . . My strong arm has overthrown (those) who came to exalt themselves: The Peleset, the Denyen and the Shekelesh.[56]

The text then puts the following words into the mouths of each group of captives, who are labelled in three registers, the top group being presumably the Shekelesh:

> Words spoken by the leaders of every country who are in the grasp of his majesty: "Great is thy strength, O mighty King, great sun of Egypt! Greater is (thy) sword than a mountain of metal, while the awe of thee is like (that of) Baal."[57]

Their reference to Baal here can only mean that he is their god, while the reference to the Pharaoh's sword's being more powerful than a mountain of metal is a way of saying that the Egyptians were more powerful than the Asiatics.

Another document from this period is the South Stela carrying the date of year 12. It is badly damaged but nevertheless is explicit and enlightening:

Year 12 under the majesty of Horus. . . . I have overthrown
the plains and hill-countries which transgressed my frontier
since I (was established) as King upon the throne of Atum.
No land was left (to) lift themselves up (in rivalry) in my
presence, while I am established like a bull before them,
sharp of horns. I caused the Asiatics (Sttyw) to turn back who
were treading Egypt . . . worn out for terror of me. They
recall my name to cause (terror) in their lands; trembling
. . . at my battle-cry, while I am a strong wall. . . . I
overthrew the Thek(er), the land of Pele(set), the Denyen,
the (W)eshesh and the Shekelesh; I destroyed the breath of
the Mesh(wesh) . . . devastated in their (own) land. . . . I
caused that they be made prostrate. I lifted up the face of
Egypt which had been downcast. . . . [58]

We find here that the Asiatics are equated to the peoples
named in the text who have been defeated on their own lands
after having crossed the frontier of Egypt. The Asiatics are
accused of rebellion and of setting themselves up "in rivalry"
towards Egypt, though we are not told exactly how. This passage
is followed by some lines, reminiscent of other texts, referring to
the peace which followed in Egypt after the defeat of the attackers
of her frontier.

There is never any suggestion that the Asiatics wanted to live
in Egypt. The texts say this only of the Libyans: " 'We will dwell
in Egypt' they say with one accord, and they kept penetrating the
frontiers of Egypt."[59] Yet we do find close co-operation between
the two groups.

The poem on the Libyan War of Year Eleven tells us that these
troubles which Egypt had been having had not always been so
pressing.

There were (no) rebels in distant lands formerly; they had
not been seen since (the time of) the kings; (but they were)
coming (in) supplication together, bearing their tribute,
doing homage and kissing the ground to him as (to) (Baal).
Their heart and their legs moved away from their lands; their
place shifted, they were not settled and all their limbs
hurried them to themselves, as if there were a stick behind
them, to sue for peace. . . . They schemed to plot rebellion a
second time, to finish their lifetime on the frontier of Egypt.
. . . The heart of his majesty stormed like Baal in the
heavens. . . . [60]

This text suggests that the Asiatics who had settled in the
Delta had themselves been driven out of their former homelands;

both physically and politically, it would appear, as their hearts went with their legs along the road to exile. This would explain the presence of the Asiatic communities in the Delta, although we cannot yet date them for the lack of evidence of this kind, so far. Nevertheless, this would also explain the common cause of the Asiatics with the Libyans during the Ramesside period. There can be no doubt that the unifying factor between these peoples was their hostility towards Egypt and their need to survive in such close proximity to this country which kept trying to drive them away from her bordering territories. It is interesting to note that in the eleventh line of the inscription of year 8, when the Pharaoh is recorded as having brought Djahy under subjection, he claims the protection of the Asiatic goddesses Anath and Astarte.[61]

The documents never leave one in any doubt that the attackers of Egypt were known to the Egyptians and that they were known to each other as well. It is a pity that we cannot yet recognize for certain the names on the Egyptian lists of enemies. With regard to the so-called Sea Peoples, we have the added problem that the names we find on the Egyptian records are probably vulgarized Egyptian versions of the original Asiatic names.

The Papyrus Harris[62]

In the last part of the Papyrus Harris, which refers to the political events in the lifetime of the recently departed Pharaoh Ramesses III, we have some details about those troubled times (and possibly earler times as well) which we do not find anywhere else. It is important as further proof that the attackers of Egypt at this time were Asiatics.

The document is presumed to have been prepared by the departed Pharaoh's son in praise of his father's deeds and achievements and in the hope that his father would intercede for him with the gods for a long and prosperous reign on earth. We must assume that this is an accurate account of events, because of the nature of the document. Yet the information it gives us appears fragmentary, and it is expressed in a sober and laconic style which contrasts markedly with the documents of the previous reign.

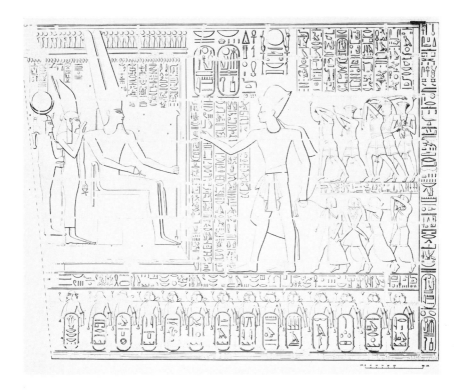

Plate I: Ramesses III presenting captives of the Libyans and the Sea Peoples to the Theban Triad, from the Mortuary Temple of Ramesses III. Below are fourteen names of enemies written as usual inside the name-ring. The list is unique in that it does not follow any of the regular patterns for the listing of the Nine Bows, nor does it resemble any other list that we have at present.

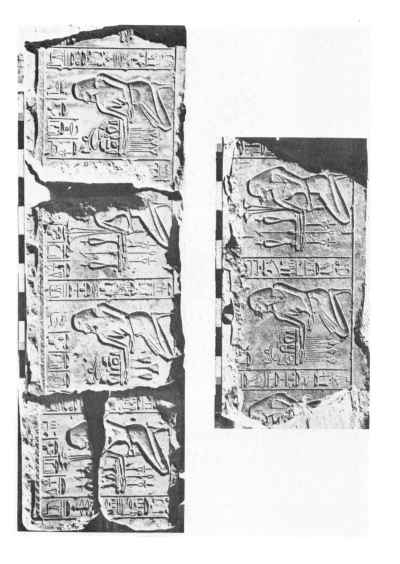

Plate II: From the Mortuary Temple of Ramesses III, some limestone reliefs show w3ḏ-wr among other figures of plenty, associated with the Nile.

Plate III. More limestone reliefs showing w3d̲-wr.

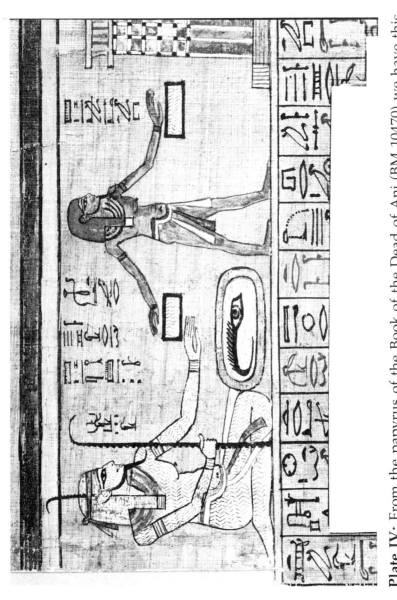

Plate IV: From the papyrus of the Book of the Dead of Ani (BM 10470) we have this beautiful drawing of w3d-wr personified and related to Ḥeḥ of a million years.

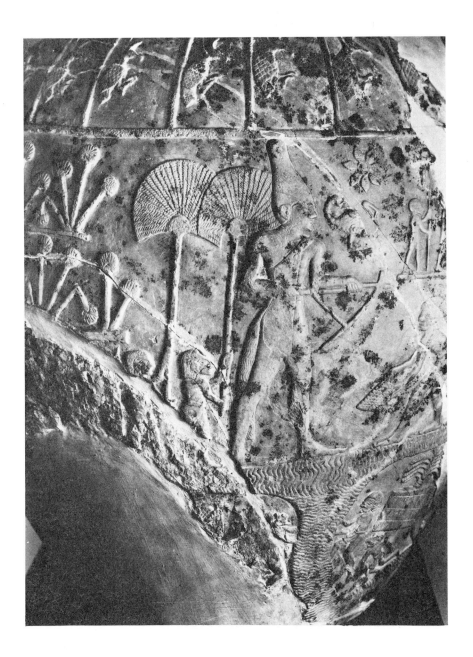

Plate V: The well-known "Scorpion" mace-head in the Ashmolean Museum (E3632) carries reliefs of the earliest representations of the papyrus plant that we have. It shows the varying thicknesses of the sudd, or underwater rhizome and root system.

Plate VI: Four islands are visible in this damaged part of the "Scorpion" mace-head and they appear to be inhabited by bearded men, possibly Asiatics. The islands are clearly portrayed as being under the feet of the Pharaoh as were the Nine Bows in later times, shown on the base of the throne and on the sandals of the Pharoah. The boat is "foreign" in shape and obviously necessary for communication between the islands. The domed shrine (at the very bottom) which may be compared with the Sobekh shrine on the swampy island shown in the tomb of Neuserre (see Fig. 16), possibly also has Asiatic connections.

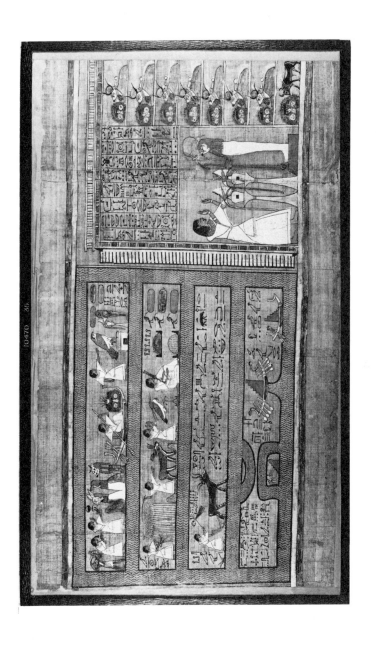

Plate VII: Again from the Book of the Dead of Ani we have islands and activities in the after-life which can only have taken their patterns from real life.

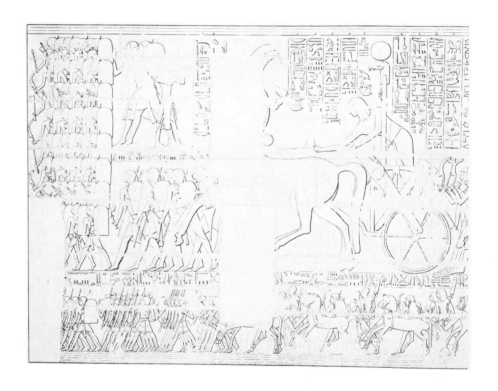

Plate VIII: In the scene showing the Pharaoh and his troops setting out to fight the Libyans, we unexpectedly find on the bottom register contingents of so-called Sea Peoples together with the Egyptians and Nubians.

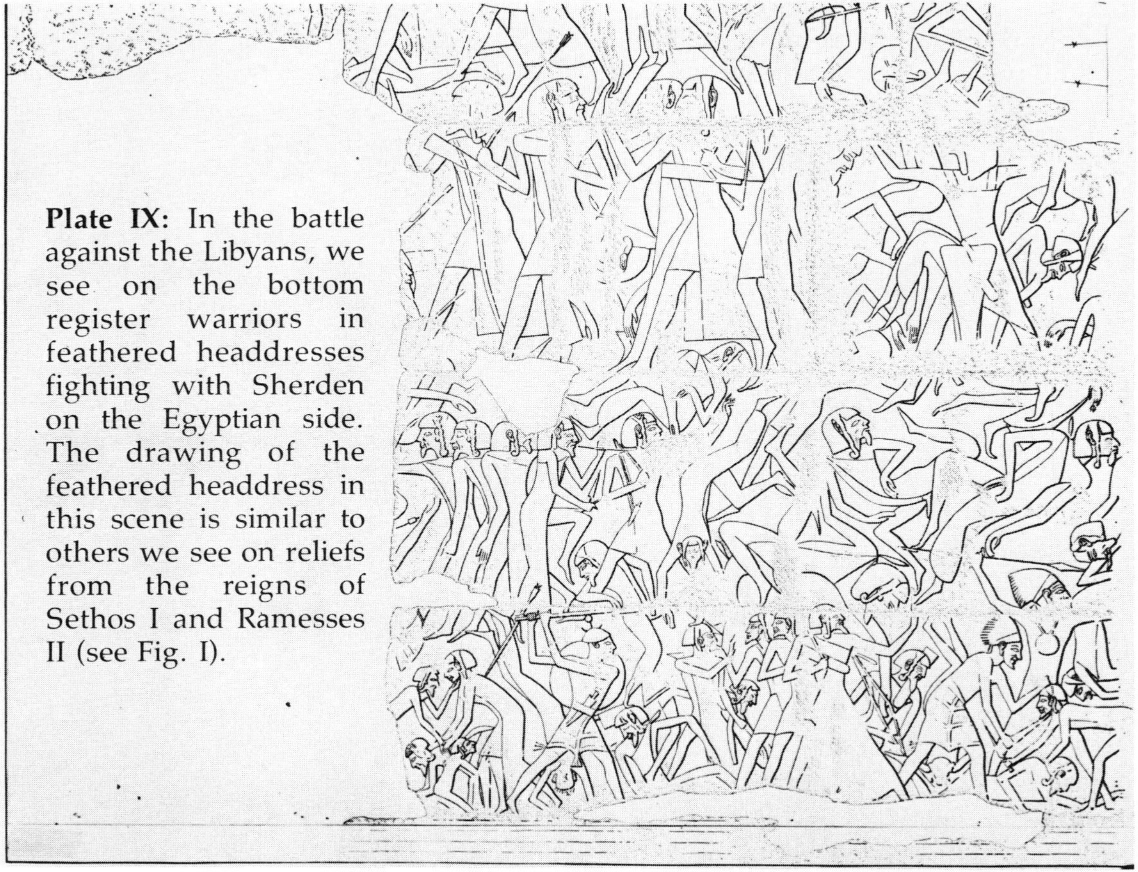

Plate IX: In the battle against the Libyans, we see on the bottom register warriors in feathered headdresses fighting with Sherden on the Egyptian side. The drawing of the feathered headdress in this scene is similar to others we see on reliefs from the reigns of Sethos I and Ramesses II (see Fig. I).

Plate X: Among the Egyptian-troops fighting against the Libyans we see in the lower register Peleset in full feathered headgear, fighting on the Egyptian side.

Plate XI: We also see Peleset fighting on the Egyptian side in the battle against the Nubians, in a relief which is now very damaged.

Plate XII: This scene represents an Egyptian attack on an Asiatic town, believed to be Tunip. This town is clearly depicted as an island with water around it. This is the way in which the Egyptian reliefs always show Asiatic towns. See also "the town of Canaan," Fig. 18. Trees are always shown in association with these towns. In this scene the Egyptians are shown to be cutting down the trees of the town and setting fire to the corn, represented by the symmetrical semicircular heaps in the fields this side of the trees.

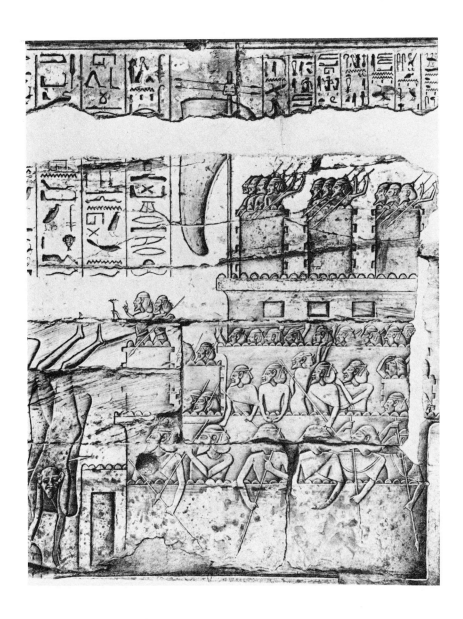

Plate XIII: A fortress in Amurru, the stronghold of the Asiatic rebels attacking Egypt, the so-called Sea Peoples.

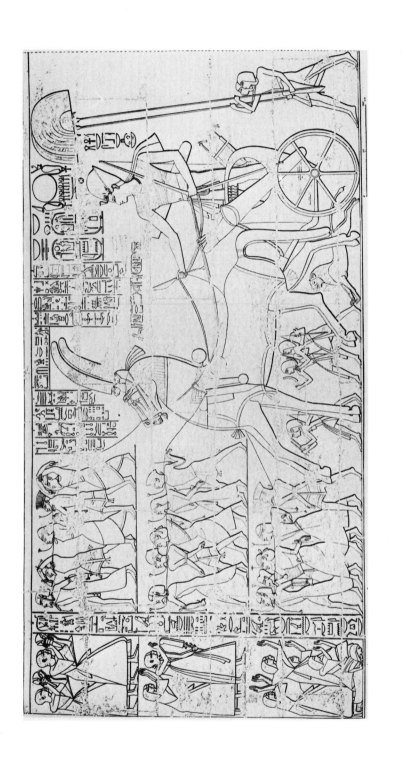

Plate XIV: Here we see the various Asiatic enemy groups being brought back as prisoners to Egypt after their defeat at Amurru.

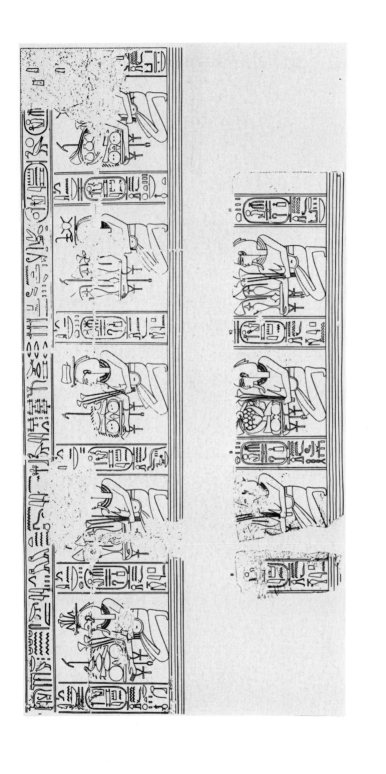

Plate XV: A relief from the Mortuary Temple at Medinet Habu stating w3d-wr to be firmly associated with the waters of the Nile.

Plate XVI: The very well-known battle on the water between the attacking forces and the Egyptians, usually called the Sea Battle. The text leaves us in no doubt that it took place on a canal.

There is a striking passage in which Ramesses III is represented as speaking to the princes and leaders of the land, the infantry and chariotry, the Sherden friendly towards Egypt, numerous archers and all the citizens of the land of Egypt:

> Hear ye, that I may inform you of my benefactions which I did while I was King of the people. The land of Egypt was (overthrown from without) and every man was (thrown out) of his right; they had no chief mouth for many years formerly until other times. The land of Egypt was in the hands of the chiefs and rulers of towns; one slew his neighbour great and small. Other times having come after it, with empty years, Yarsu, a certain Syrian was with them as chief. He set the whole land tributary before him together; he united his companions and plundered their possessions. They made the gods like men and no offerings were presented in the temples.[63]

We do not know what period these lines refer to, although we are told later that it was Sethnakht, the predecessor of Ramesses III who set things right in the land of Egypt and that Ramesses III had carried on this work.

The period of disorder described here when petty princes, chiefs and rulers of towns had ruled Egypt without any reference to the common good fits very well into the picture we have of the relationship of the western Asian city states as reflected, for example, in the Amarna period.[64] There can be no doubt that the disorders reflect the work of Asiatic rulers, warring among themselves and bringing their problems into Egypt.

It is possible that this passage is referring to the ancient troubles with the Hyksos rulers. If this is so, then the only point in mentioning them in this document would be that they were related to the events which took place in the lifetime of Ramesses III. There are many reasons, including this passage, which suggest that we must see the attacks on Egypt during the Ramesside period as a continuation and another climax, perhaps, of her endemic troubles with her Asiatic neighbours.

If the above-quoted passage is not referring to the Hyksos period, then what is described is a recurrence of a similar situation which prompted the vigorous and decisive intervention by Ramesses III.

Dr. Faulkner has said that it need not be assumed that conditions in Egypt were quite as chaotic as this document seems to suggest because it followed a convention which showed conditions to be bad in order to throw a dramatic light on the subsequent improvements.[65] However, the account in Papyrus Harris is not a dramatic one. It is in a subdued key. No details are given of a situation which must have been very serious indeed, namely, hostile people right on Egypt's borders, and preparing to attack her. Nor do the main statements appear to be at all laboured. It seems very odd that only these scanty facts are given in a general resumé of the recent history of Egypt, even though we are told that Ramesses III was only instrumental in carrying on the good work of Sethnakht.[66]

When the Pharaoh is made to speak of his military achievements in this document, he says that he has extended all the boundaries of Egypt, overthrowing *in their own lands* those who had invaded his country:

> I extended all the boundaries of Egypt; I overthrew those who invaded them in their lands. I slew the Denyen in their isles, the Thekel and the Peleset were made ashes. The Sherden and the Weshesh of the ym they were made as those that exist not, taken captive at one time, brought as captives to Egypt, like the sands of the shore. I settled them in strongholds, bound in my name. . . . I taxed them all, in clothing and in grain from the store-houses and granaries each year.[67]

Here again we are told explicitly that the invaders of Egypt's frontier were defeated in their own lands, the Pharaoh extending his own frontier through these victories.

Dr. Faulkner drew attention to the fact that the historical section of this long and carefully prepared papyrus makes no mention of the war in Syria, recorded so dramatically at Medinet Habu. This would indeed be a remarkable omission in a document which records in some detail the defeat of the people of Seir (the Shosu-Beduin) and the war against the Libyans.

But the war in Syria is recorded. It is referred to in the passage we quoted above, in which the Denyen, Thekel and Peleset were said to have been defeated in their own lands. While the exact identity of these peoples is still not clear except in a general way as Asiatics, and the Peleset as Philistines, we are left in no doubt at all as to where their settlements lay, adjoining the Egyptian frontier. We have already said that we believe much of the fighting was due to Asiatic settlements in the Delta which is where we believe the area of Retenu or Djahy to have begun.

There are several similar statements at Medinet Habu, written in the lifetime of Ramesses III, in which the defeat of the enemy is mentioned together with his extension of Egypt's boundaries, so that we can safely take this to be true.

There is no real evidence for the statement by Dr. Faulkner[68] that the various states of Syria had ceased to exist as political entities at this time. The Temple at Medinet Habu has many scenes showing the defeat of the Asiatics or Syrians on their home ground and they are certainly mentioned in the texts of the time as being a real threat to Egypt. But if anyone needed further proof of Asiatic vigour at this time it can be found in the Papyrus Harris in the passage where Ramesses III is made to describe the peace which enveloped Egypt when the enemy was finally defeated by him:

> I made the woman of Egypt go . . . to the place she desired, (for) no stranger nor anyone upon the road molested her. I made the infantry and chariotry to dwell (at home) in my time; the Sherden and Kehek were in their towns, lying the length of their backs; they had no fear, (for) there was no enemy from Kush, (nor) foes from Syria. Their bows and their weapons reposed in their magazines, while they were satisfied and drunk with joy. . . . [69]

Only two peoples are mentioned here as the enemies Egypt had to contend with during the lifetime of Ramesses III. They are the people of the southern area of Kush and the northern people of Syria. One would expect these to represent the areas from which Egypt expected hostilities. No other attackers are mentioned in this, a summary of the main events in the period of the reign of Ramesses III.

Attention should perhaps be drawn to the statement that the Pharaoh had worked hard to restore the whole land for the benefit of all, including foreigners, who come quite high on the list of those sharing in the new prosperity abounding in the land.[70] It is important to remember that these foreigners can only be the people over whom Egypt claimed sovereignty, former rebels and former enemies, probably including the settlements of the Delta.

The Papyrus concludes with an exhortation to all to venerate and obey the present ruler, Ramesses IV, as they do the god Re: "Present to him your tribute (in) his august palace, bring to him the gifts of the lands and countries."[71]

Egypt's enemies may have been defeated, but not to the extent that they would be unable to continue to bring gifts and tribute to the Pharaoh.

The Earlier Attack in the Reign of Merenptah

We have four inscriptions informing us about the attacks on Egypt during the time of Merenptah, the long Karnak inscription,[72] the "Athribis" Stela,[73] the Cairo Column,[74] and the "Hymn of Victory,"[75] also called the "Israel" Stela.

There can be no doubt that all four documents refer to the same events because they all carry the same definite date. The Israel Stela begins by referring to "year 5, third month of the third season, day 3," which corresponds exactly to the date given on the Athribis Stela concerning the date of the battle in which the invaders were defeated, although we know from the Cairo fragment that the attackers had crossed the frontiers of Egypt a whole month before this time. The Karnak inscription also tells us that the armies were ready in their camps on "the night of the second day of the third month of the third season" waiting for the day to break.[76]

To this exact date is added the further information in three of the texts that the attackers, named in the Karnak inscription as Sherden, Shekelesh, Ekwesh, Lukka and Turush, were closely allied to the Libyans. The Karnak inscription refers to the "list of captives carried off from this land of Libya and the countries which he brought with him"[77] and lists them in detail calling them northerners. The Athribis inscription lists the same people, after which the Libyan women and the plunder are mentioned, while the Cairo column begins the list at a point where the stone is broken off.

The Israel Stela does not list Egypt's enemies by the same names as those in the other texts, although it records the same events, in considerable detail, and carries the same date. In its concluding lines, we have references to Egypt's already well-known enemies in the countries north of Egypt, together with the Libyans: the princes (Asiatics) who say "shalom," the Nine Bows, the Tehenu (Libyans), the Canaan, Ashkelon, Gezer, Yanoam, Israel and Hurru. As a result of this victory, we are told, Hatti is at peace. There is no reason to suppose that the last few lines of this stela are unrelated to the rest.

It has often been suggested that the Israel Stela is a poetic eulogy of the universally victorious Pharaoh.[78] There are one or two general passages in the text. But it is otherwise a meticulously detailed account of the battle on the day. After the usual abundant praise for the King in its opening lines, it goes on to tell us:

> The wretched enemy prince of Rebu was fled in the depth of night, by himself. No feather was on his head; his feet were unshod. His women were taken before his face. The loaves for his provision were seized; he had no water of the waterskin to keep him alive.[79]

There is a great deal of such detail in this Stela, too much of it to be claimed that it is a universal and general statement of victory by the Pharaoh.

Since all four documents carry the same date and the longer ones all give details of the same battle, one must accept that they all refer to the same enemies on that occasion. Had we not had the other documents, we would have had to assume that the enemies listed at the end of the Israel Stela referred to the events in the main body of the document. However, because of the names used in the other three texts, it has always been assumed that the concluding lines of the Israel Stela are a general summary of Egypt's troubles rather than one of a particular occasion. Yet it is most likely that this was just another event in Egypt's constantly recurring hostilities with her Asiatic northern neighbours.

One of the other documents recording this event, the Karnak inscription, speaks in line 18 of the "invasion of every (hill-) country while the Nine Bows plunder its borders and rebels invade it every day . . . ." It goes on to say:

> They have repeatedly penetrated the fields of Egypt on the (great) river . . . they have spent whole days and months dwelling . . . . They have reached the hills of the oasis . . . . (So) it has been since the Kings of Upper Egypt, in the records of other times . . . .[80]

In other words, the invasion of Egypt's borders by foreigners was nothing new at all. These lines suggest that the invasion may have consisted of a descent from the Delta by the foreign groups, as they had done from time immemorial. They also suggest that Egypt's boundary lay somewhere near the Nile proper, before it split up into streams.

The Israel Stela refers to the princes (wrw) who were overthrown, namely Asiatic princes. These princes are made to say
"shalom," which confirms their Semitic origin. Breasted noted
that the conquered enemy in Ramesses III's fifth year used the
same Semitic greeting.[81] The word "shalom" would not otherwise be used naturally by the Egyptian scribe.

We have another clue in these texts that the enemy were
western Asiatics by the number of references to Baal/Seth. In the
Karnak text we find in line 69: "Baal gives victory and might to
Horus. . . . " In the Athribis monument, line 7 tells us: " . . .
the fallen of Libya . . . whom Amon-Re and Baal gave (to) King
Merenptah . . . . " The Israel Stela says in line 11 that the Libyans
are defeated and have lost their power in Egypt "for Baal has
turned his back upon their chief, their settlements are aban-
doned. . . . " It is asserted that the enemy's own god has
deserted them. This is in keeping with the general Egyptian
practice of honouring the gods of their enemies in the hope that
they may protect the Pharaoh.

Baal came to share exactly the same determinative with Seth
in the New Kingdom. Seth/Baal was the god of the foreign
countries, and Dr. Te Velde points out[82] that it was specially in
the circles of the colonial army that Seth was held in honour.

Another indication that Egypt's attackers at this time were
Semitic northerners is to be found in the Karnak inscription
where the list of captives and slain shows the Libyans to be
uncircumcised while their allies were recorded as having "no
foreskins." The consequence of this was that their hands were
cut off for the reckoning, instead of their phalli, as was the case
with the Libyans. The Athribis Stela confirms these same details.
We find no mention of circumcision in the later Ramesside texts.

Lastly the point should be emphasized which was first
mentioned by Sir Flinders Petrie in 1905[83] that, for nomadic
tribes, the Libyans and their allies had a remarkable quantity of
valuable objects as the lists of spoil show. Not only did they have
a great stock of cattle and goats, impossible to move with any
speed, but also horses, weapons and silver drinking vessels, as
well as leather tents. The Egyptians themselves obviously felt
that they did very well with their plunder on this occasion
because they inscribed the details of it so carefully on their public
monuments. We know that Syria and Libya were great producers
of cattle at this time and that Egypt imported a great deal of

livestock from these countries. We also know that the northern countries were particularly skilled in metalwork and so did the Egyptians, because they make a feature of the Sherden and the Meshwesh swords in their texts and their pictures.

As for the Meshwesh, we have long known about their "copper swords." But the late Dr. W. C. Hayes in 1951 drew attention to an inscription on a jar from the time of Amenophis III which contained "fat from the bulls of the Meshwesh" showing that their skills extended to animal husbandry, at a much earlier date than this.[84]

There can be no doubt that the records from the reign of Ramesses II, Merenptah's father, can enlighten us considerably concerning the attacks on Egypt during his son's reign. In his lifetime there had been attacks on Egypt's frontier too. It is interesting to find Ashkelon mentioned among the enemies transgressing Egypt's frontier then:

> The wretched town which his majesty took when it was wicked, Ashkelon. It says: "Happy is he who acts in fidelity to thee, (but) woe (to) him who transgresses thy frontier! Leave over a heritage, so that we may relate thy strength to every ignorant foreign country!"[85]

In line 39 of the Great Abydos Inscription there is a reference to this Pharaoh, "the fear of whom expels foreign lands."[86] On one of the rock side-walls of the Bet El-Walli Temple,[87] the remains of an inscription over the enemy reads: " . . . those who trangress his boundaries." We have already referred to the passage in the Aswân Stela where Ramesses II is said to have "crushed the foreigners of the north, the Temeh have fallen for fear of him, the Asiatics are anxious for breath from him. . . . "[88] It is in this same passage that the ruler is recorded as having plundered the warriors of the Great Green without any reference to a naval battle or to an attack on the part of the enemy.

A re-consideration of these texts together with those from the reign of Ramesses III may well bring us all to the conclusion that Egypt's attackers were in fact her traditional enemies, called at this time more accurately by the names of the towns from which they came, because by now, the Egyptians knew them better than they did before. The problem remains to identify these names from the Asiatic areas north of Egypt. We cannot do this yet without a great deal of speculation.

It is possible that the pictorial record can help us a little, but we do not yet have enough information to discuss this aspect of the problem satisfactorily.

NOTES ON CHAPTER FOUR

Chapter Four in this book is substantially the same as Chapters Four and Five in the author's earlier publication: *The Sea Peoples: A Re-Examination of the Egyptian Sources*, Oxford, 1972.

Unless otherwise stated, all the plates referred to in this chapter are from the Oriental Institute, University of Chicago: *Medinet Habu*, 1930-1970.

The following abbreviated references are used in this chapter:

Breasted	J. Breasted, *Ancient Records of Egypt* (Chicago, 1906).
Edgerton and Wilson	W.F. Edgerton and J.A. Wilson, *Historical Records of Ramesses III* (Chicago, 1936).
Erichsen	W. Erichsen, *Papyrus Harris I, Hieroglyphische Transkription,* Bibliotheca Aegyptiaca, V (Brussels, 1933).
Faulkner	R.O. Faulkner, "Egypt, from the Inception of the Nineteenth Dynasty to the Death of Ramesses III," *Cambridge Ancient History, II,* Chapter XXIII.
Gardiner	A.H. Gardiner, *Ancient Egyptian Onomastica* (Oxford, 1947).
Helck	H.W. Helck, *Die Beziehungen Ägyptens zu Vorderasien im 3. und 2. Jahrtausend v. Chr.* (Wiesbaden, 1971²).
Kitchen	K.A. Kitchen, *Ramesside Inscriptions* (Oxford, 1968-).
Rowton	M.B. Rowton, "The Woodlands of Ancient Western Asia," *Journal of Near Eastern Studies* (1967).
Wilson	J.A. Wilson, trans., in J.B. Pritchard, ed., *Ancient Near Eastern Texts Relating to the Old Testament* (Princeton, 1969³).

1. Plate 46; Edgerton and Wilson, pp. 49f.
2. Plate 44; Edgerton and Wilson, p. 48.
3. Plate 46; Edgerton and Wilson, p. 53.
4. Wilson, p. 251.
5. Plate 123 A; Edgerton and Wilson, p. 151.
6. R.D. Barnett, "The Sea Peoples," *Cambridge Ancient History*, vol. II, chapter XXVIII, III.
7. Helck, pp. 230f.
8. N. de G. Davis and R.O. Faulkner, "A Syrian Trading Venture to Egypt," *Journal of Egyptian Archaeology*, XXXIII, plate VIII.
9. R. Kupper, *Les Nomades en Mesopotamie au temps des rois de Mari* (Paris, 1957).
10. J. Koenig, "La Revanche d'Amurru sur Babel," *Ugaritica VI* (Paris, 1969).

11. J. Van Seters, *The Hyksos* (New Haven, 1966), chapter 13.

12. K. Sethe, *Die Ächtung feindlicher Fürsten* (Berlin, 1926); G. Posener, *Princes et pays d'Asie et de Nubie* (Bruxelles, 1940); also, "Les Textes d'Envoûtement de Mirgissa," *Syria,* XLIII (1966): 277ff.

13. Gardiner, vol. I, pp. 188*f.

14. *Medinet Habu,* plate 600 B.

15. J.F. Champollion, *Grammaire égyptienne* (1836), p. 180.

16. Plate 46; Edgerton and Wilson, pp. 54f.

17. We are taking the view in this text that "Great Green" means a part of the Delta so that the enemy were dragged on to land out of the canal water.

18. Plate 56; Edgerton and Wilson, pp. 54f.

19. See Chapter Two for a discussion of Retenu.

21. Plate 46; Edgerton and Wilson, pp. 57f.

22. Rowton, pp. 265f.

23. Rowton, p. 266.

24. Wilson, pp. 239f.

25. Plate 88.

26. Wilson, pp. 240f.

27. Plates 27-28; Edgerton and Wilson, pp. 19ff.

28. Edgerton and Wilson, p. 23.

29. Edgerton and Wilson, p. 24.

30. Edgerton and Wilson, p. 24.

31. Edgerton and Wilson, p. 27.

32. Edgerton and Wilson, p. 30.

33. Edgerton and Wilson, p. 32.

34. Edgerton and Wilson, p. 34.

35. Plate 16; Edgerton and Wilson, p. 7.

36. Plate 23; Edgerton and Wilson, p. 16.

37. Plate 14; Edgerton and Wilson, p. 6.

38. Plate 29; Edgerton and Wilson, pp. 35f.

39. Plate 29; Edgerton and Wilson, p. 37.

40. Plates 32-34.

41. Edgerton and Wilson, pp. 38f.

42. Plates 37-39.

43. Plate 37; Edgerton and Wilson, p. 41.

44. Plate 37; Edgerton and Wilson, p. 41.

45. Plate 42; Edgerton and Wilson, p. 43.

46. W. Wolf, "Der Berliner Ptah-Hymnus" (P 3048, II-XII), *ZÄS* 64 (1929): 17ff, line 29.

47. Plate 43; Edgerton and Wilson, pp. 44f.

48. Plate 43; Edgerton and Wilson, p. 46.

49. Plate 43; Edgerton and Wilson, p. 46.

50. Edgerton and Wilson, p. 46, Note 30a.

51. Plate 43; Edgerton and Wilson, p. 45.

52. Plate 44; lines 14-15.

53. The Hymn of Victory, also called the Israel Stela: Kitchen, IV, 3a,b, 12; Wilson, p. 376.

54. Plate 44.

55. Plate 44; lines 14-15.

56. Plate 44; Edgerton and Wilson, p. 48.

57. Plate 44; lines 18-20.

58. Plate 107; Edgerton and Wilson, pp. 130f.

59. Plate 80; Edgerton and Wilson, p. 76f.

60. Plates 85-86; Edgerton and Wilson, p. 89.

61. Plate 80; line 11.

62. See Erichsen; also Breasted, vol. IV.

63. Breasted, pars. 397ff.; also Faulkner, section XI.

64. G. Buccellati, *Cities and Nations of Ancient Syria* (Rome, 1967): Studi Semitici 26.

65. Faulkner, section XI.

66. Breasted, vol. IV, par. 399.

67. Breasted, vol. IV, par. 403.

68. Faulkner, section XII.

69. Breasted, vol. IV, par. 410; Erichsen, I, 78, pp. 9f.

70. Breasted, vol. IV, par. 410; Erichsen, I, 78, pp. 13f.

71. Breasted, vol. IV, par. 412; Erichsen, I, 79, p. 9.

72. Kitchen, IV, 2, 2; Breasted, vol. III, pars. 572ff.

73. Kitchen, IV, 19; Breasted, vol. III, pars. 596ff.

74. Kitchen, IV, 5, 23; Breasted, vol. III, pp. 593f.

75. Kitchen, IV, 3a,b I2; Breasted, vol. III, pp. 602f; also Wilson, pp. 376f.

76. Line 31.

77. Line 48.

78. Helck, p. 224; also E. Uphill, "The Nine Bows," *Jaarbericht Ex Oriente Lux*, 19 (1967): 399f.

79. Wilson, p. 377.

80. Breasted, vol. III, par. 580.

81. Breasted, vol. III, p. 263, note f; also vol. IV, par. 43, line 50; and vol. IV, par. 45, line 56.

82. H. Te Velde, *Seth, The God of Confusion* (Leiden, 1967), pp. 134f; also J. Gwyn Griffiths, *The Conflict between Horus and Seth* (Liverpool, 1960), p. 48.

83. W. Flinders Petrie, *A History of Egypt* (London, 1924⁷) vol. III, pp. 107f.

84. W.C. Hayes, "Inscriptions from the Palace of Amenhotep III," *Journal of Near Eastern Studies,* X (1951): 91.

85. Wilson, p. 256.

86. Breasted, vol. III, par. 265, line 39.

87. Breasted, vol. III, par. 474.

88. Gardiner, vol. I, p. 195*.

The Pictorial Record

With the exception of a reference to the Lukka in a Byblos obelisk dedicated to Reseph[1] and in some Hittite records which we have already mentioned,[2] it is a significant fact that all the records we have telling us about the so-called Sea Peoples come from Egypt, including the cuneiform letters from Tell el-Amarna. However, the pictorial record is not confined to Egypt although it is only from Medinet Habu that we have a row of prisoners which are explicitly called "the northern countries" and which are also labelled specifically by the names of the attackers that we find in the texts (frontispiece B). We are very lucky to have this valuable relief, which, though damaged, still gives us considerable detail, clearly having the purpose of instructing the Egyptian viewer on how the enemies of the northern countries looked. The sculptor of these reliefs went to some lengths to show racial differences in the faces of these prisoners, as well as distinguishing them by their headgear.

This relief is of great importance because not only does it state beyond any dispute that the northern countries were the hill-countries immediately to the north of Egypt, but also because it portrays so clearly the headgear of these enemies that we are able to recognise it as familiar and as having been shown in the reliefs of earlier periods.

Plate I shows us from left to right, which is the way they are facing: the prince of Khatti, the prince of Amurru, the chieftain of the Tjekker, a Sherden of the water, the chieftain of the

Figure 13. Ox-carts, women and children from the land battle with the Sea Peoples. Here is one of the only two *bearded* Sherden found in the Egyptian reliefs. His helmet is shown here to be built up in layers suggesting that it could have been made of leather.

Sh(ekelesh), a Turush of the water, while the last label, beginning to spell out Peleset, has also lost the figure for this racial
type, so it is to some extent an assumption when we call the
figures with the feathered headdresses Philistines.

We cannot ordinarily rely on a literal interpretation of the
Egyptian reliefs, because it may happen that Shekelesh, Denyen
and Peleset are mentioned in detail in the texts whereas only the
enemy in the "feathered" (reed or horsehair?)[3] headdresses
appear in the pictorial version of the story.[4] Undoubtedly these
and the Sherden are the most pictorially satisfying of all the
attackers and we may excuse the artist for choosing to show
enemies wearing their apparel. For years, centuries in fact, the
Egyptian artist had been portraying ordinary Asiatics in their
prosaic gear. It is these two colourful groups only who are
portrayed in both the "Sea" and the "Land" battles at Medinet
Habu. The Sherden had already appeared with spectacular effect
in the scenes of the Battle of Qadesh in the temples at Luxor,
Karnak, Abydos and Abu Simbel.

Among the many scenes portraying the hostilities between
the Egyptians and their attackers on the walls of the Mortuary
Temple of Ramesses III at Medinet Habu, it is the scenes of the
"Sea" and "Land" battles which have received most attention by
scholars. The pictorial record itself, quite apart from the texts,
which we have already discussed, has given rise to much
speculation and misinterpretation.

In the case of the Land Battle[5] it seemed at first that the many
ox-carts depicted were very foreign with their solid wooden
wheels and pulled, as they were shown, by humped oxen (fig.
13). It was also thought that because women and children were
present in these carts accompanying the warriors, they represented a migration of peoples. Dr. Y. Yadin has now shown
that these ox-carts are identical with those still in use today in
Anatolia and in the Middle East.[6] It is now also quite clear from
the Egyptian texts and illustrations that it was the custom of Near
Eastern princes to take their families with them whenever they
travelled abroad. They had to come to Egypt periodically with
their tribute and on these occasions they travelled with their
families, sometimes having to leave their children behind at the
Pharaoh's court (fig. 14).

As for the humped oxen, Helck has drawn attention to the fact
that such animals are shown pictorially in the tomb of Kenamun

Figure 14. From the tomb of Menkheperrasonb (N. de G. Davies), this scene shows Asiatics bringing tribute, including children, as is often shown in the eighteenth dynasty tombs.

and elsewhere,[7] proving that they were not unknown in Egypt, where the records show a great quantity of cattle to have come from the Near Eastern countries and Libya.

In the scene of the so-called Sea Battle, a careful examination of the pictorial material will show it to have taken place very close to land, so much so that some Egyptian bowmen on land are shooting at the enemy in the boats.[8] We have already drawn attention to the text which states the fighting to have taken place in the mouths of the Nile, in or on the Great Green.

The boats themselves are so schematically shown that they cannot reveal any positive provenance.[9]

In both battles, the enemy all use round shields and both groups are shown to use two weapons, the spear and the long dagger or sword (Plate XVI).

It must be stressed that there are some quite unexpected scenes among this pictorial material. For example, where the reliefs show the Pharaoh and his troops to be fighting the Nubians, we find on the much-damaged surface at least two warriors in feathered headdresses left in the melee (Plate XI). It is not clear which side they are fighting on, but there are no feathered headdresses among the Nubian captives presented to Amon and Mut.[10]

In the scene showing Ramesses III setting out with his army to fight the Libyans,[11] we are surprised to find contingents of bearded Asiatics, together with Sherden, Peleset and Nubians (Plate VIII). The scene of the battle against the Libyans clearly shows Peleset and Sherden fighting on the Egyptian side as they are drawn killing Libyans (Plate IX).

We find a similar portrayal of foreign contingents in the lion hunt[12] and again in the scene showing Ramesses III setting out for Djahi (or Zahi) with his troops to fight the Sea Peoples,[13] (fig. 15).

It is perhaps worth noting that the Sherden fighting on the side of Egypt usually appear to have the disc on their helmets while those fighting against her do not. This could possibly be a symbol of allegiance to Re. In the Land Battle where some Sherden are fighting on the Egyptian side, this distinction is made. However, the Sherden prisoner on the labelled list shown in our Plate I is shown in the way most familiar to the Egyptians, with the disc on his helmet, although he is presented as an enemy. He is also shown bearded there, which is not usual for this enemy, only one other Sherden soldier having been shown

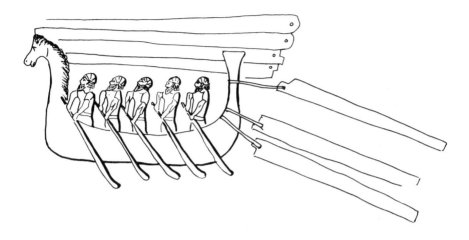

Figure 15. From the story of Wenamun it is learned that seven hewn tree trunks were the full load for a ship going to Egypt from the Lebanon. On one of the Nineveh reliefs exactly such a ship may be seen, showing the careful preparation of the logs for stacking and lashing to the ship. See *Literature of Ancient Egypt,* ed. W. Kelly Simpson, Yale, 1972, p. 151; M. Botta and M. Flandrin, *Monument de Nineveh,* Paris, 1849, plate 33.

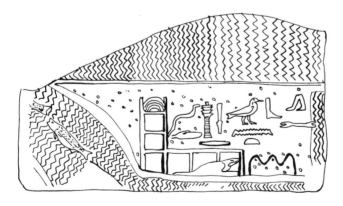

Figure 16. An island in the Delta and probably Asiatic. It is portrayed as being either swampy or misty. From the same chamber in the tomb of Neuserre as figure 9.

bearded in the reliefs, in the Land Battle (fig. 13).[14]

The helmet of this particular bearded warrior is drawn as though it were built up of layers of material. This could well be leather, as this method of building up the helmet base is suggested by other drawings, including the feathered helmets, some of which appear to have the same base as the one we have just described.

Some of the warriors in the feathered headdresses appear to be wearing a disc amulet around their necks. But the reliefs are too damaged on the whole for us to be able to determine whether this could be the equivalent of the Sherden helmet disc.[15]

We have said that these attackers of Egypt's frontier are shown pictorially for the first time in the reliefs from the reign of Ramesses III. What we really mean is that they first appear as a group under these specific names. As we have already said, the headgear in our labelled list of enemies (frontispiece) is familiar and we must emphasize that several members of this group had been shown in battle with the Egyptians in earlier times, but they were not specifically identified by name.

If we look again at the reliefs from Luxor (first pylon, east tower, outer face)[16] telling the story of Qadesh and dating from the time of Ramesses II, we see some of these same caps and some feathered headdresses as well. Our figure 17 shows from the reliefs a row of enemy soldiers depicting, from right to left as they are facing, first a Tjekker, fourth from the right, a Shekelesh; seventh, a Shosu-Beduin,[17] tenth, probably a Turush; and lastly, a Peleset (or possibly Lukka?); but undoubtedly a feathered headdress carefully cut into the rock. Moreover they are carrying spears and also daggers of exactly the same shape as those carried by the Sherden and Peleset at Medinet Habu, only drawn rather shorter in this case.

Even in the earlier reliefs of Sethos I in the Great Hypostyle Hall at Karnak, showing the fortress of "the town of Canaan," (fig. 18),[18] we see headdresses such as those worn by Shekelesh and Turush in our Plate I. In a scene showing the return of Sethos I from an Asiatic campaign, we find a row of prisoners approaching a canal filled with crocodiles, a well-known relief.[19] The text tells us that these are prisoners from the tribes of the Shosu-Beduin, who were rebelling and quarelling among themselves, but it is clear that the term as it is used here is a generic one referring to various groups of people. The headgear worn by

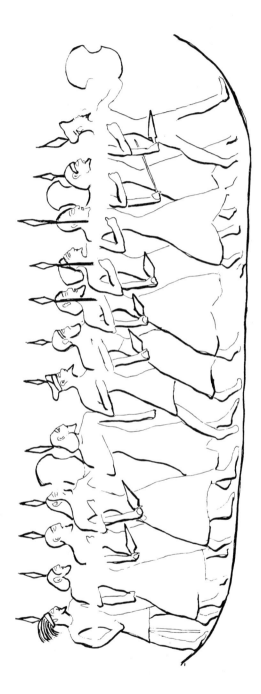

Figure 17. A row of enemy soldiers shown inside the city of Kadesh; reliefs from the time of Ramesses II at Luxor.

these tribesmen is varied and among them we distinguish some feathered kinds (fig. 1). In the Sethos I reliefs, the feathered headdresses are never drawn in the detail which we find at Medinet Habu. Often they are merely suggested by drawing a feathered outline at the end of the cap. We have some examples of this kind of drawing at Medinet Habu, but it is not common in those reliefs (Plate IX).[20] This could possibly be an earlier convention for drawing feathered headdresses, but we cannot be certain about this.

It may not seem so incredible to some people that caps such as those worn by the Shosu-Beduin and other Asiatic tribes (fig. 17) are to be recognised in the Cretan ones from seals and figurines illustrated as figure 68 by Mr. Sinclair Hood in his book, *The Minoans*.[21] Yet we are not able to explain this at present.

Egypt's attackers may sometimes be recognised in pictorial evidence from abroad but unfortunately this is never very enlightening.

We have from Phaestos in Crete the well-known disc showing beardless faces under feathered headdresses,[22] although these are not quite the same as those shown at Medinet Habu. They are obviously elements in a pictographic inscription, so far unique, dating to a Middle Minoan III context, which we are unfortunately unable to read. However, it is logical to assume that these heads must have been clearly recognisable and accepted symbols for them to have been used in this way.

From Enkomi in Cyprus, that is, from a Canaanite context, of approximately the twelfth century B.C., we have a scene showing two figures in feathered headdresses and costume, similar to that worn in the Medinet Habu reliefs, but with some variation, and they are bearded in true Semitic style, something we never find on the Egyptian reliefs (fig. 19). They appear on an ivory gaming-board together with other figures in completely different dress, taking part in an animal hunt.[23] Our two figures are shown to be moving on foot, and carrying an axe, a weapon we never see used by men in feathered headdresses on the Egyptian reliefs. They appear to be on amicable terms with the others, and all bent on a common purpose, the hunt. The fact that the gaming-board is made of ivory suggests a Near Eastern provenance, and the manner in which our two figures are portrayed shows that they are not considered as enemies, in that context at least, at that particular time.

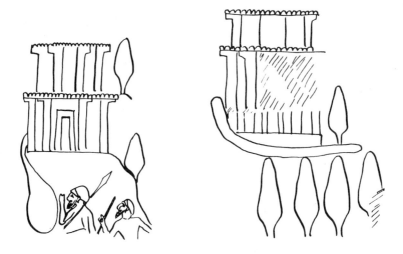

Figure 18. The towns of "Canaan" and Yanoam, portrayed by the Egyptian artist in the typical style of Asiatic towns, on a real or contrived island, surrounded by water.

Figure 19. A Peleset-type figure from an ivory gaming-board from En-komi. See H. Frankfort, *The Art and Architecture of the Ancient Orient*, 1954, p. 152; also C. Descamps de Mertzenfeld, *Ivoires phéniciennes*, Paris, 1954, plate LXIX.

From Beth-Shan, Lachish and Tell el-Farah in Palestine, a number of anthropoid clay coffins have been found showing feathered headdresses marked in considerable detail in the clay. Both Dr. Yadin, in his book,[24] and Dr. Trude Dothan, the excavator, have stressed the great detail shown in the representations of the bands holding the feathers (or other material) together. These are decorated either with a wavy band pattern or with one or two parallel rows of small circular discs (fig. 20), which are identical with those we find at Medinet Habu. It is now becoming clear from a number of excavations, as Drs. T. and M. Dothan have said,[25] that these "Philistine" anthropoid sarcophagi may be found without the presence of the so-called Philistine pottery; and, vice versa, Philistine pottery may be found without these sarcophagi. Dr. E. Oren in his recent book has described with great care his finds in the northern cemetery of Beth-Shan.[26] Many anthropoid sarcophagi showing feathered headdresses were found there, but no Philistine pottery.

Of the many Philistine sites, only Tell el-Farah has produced both anthropoid clay coffins and Philistine pottery together, but on these sarcophagi no feathered headdresses are shown.

In a most interesting paper given at the Sheffield Colloquium in 1973,[27] Dr. Lagarce pointed out that the cylinder-shaped bottle and some of the painted decorations of the so-called Philistine ware have earlier antecedants in the Cypriote ware of Enkomi and other sites.

Time may encourage us to take more seriously the proposals by Dr. Muhly that Philistine pottery may be no more than "regional variations of Mycenaean III CI pottery."[28] This could be another example of the dangers of attaching a people to a style of pottery!

Professor Schachermeyr's study of feathered and horned helmets in the Egyptian reliefs[29] is a valuable contribution to an eventual solution of these problems. However, the fact that the pictorial record from the time of Ramesses III is taken in isolation, without reference to earlier pictorial records or textual references in the Egyptian reliefs, seriously limits the range from which this problem is examined, even though Aegean comparisons are made.

As far as the Sherden are concerned, Dr. Grosjean drew our attention as far back as 1966 to the stone figures in Corsica.[30] It is striking how the detail on these stone figures is so similar to the costumes shown to be worn by the Sherden on the reliefs at Medinet Habu. It is most unfortunate that these figures, being in stone and in no obviously related context, can provide us with no dates.

Quoting again from the Sheffield Colloquium of 1973, Dr. M. Makkay presented a paper suggesting the possibility that the Sherden helmets were made of leather.[31] He drew some comparisons with helmets found in East Hungary, where the horns were of boar's tusks. It is impossible from the Egyptian reliefs to be sure of the material used in these helmets, but they may well have been of leather rather than metal, judging from some of the examples which show overlapping sections building up the crown, as we see on figure 13.

Altogether, apart from the labelled list of our frontispiece we may glean very little from the pictorial record. Yet there is no doubt that until today it has been given far too much importance in its own right, independently of the texts. We must now regain the balance necessary to consider the pictorial record only as a supplement to the content of the Egyptian texts themselves. These texts speak of "hostility" and "rebellion," never of invasion. It is therefore up to those scholars who insist on a migration and invasion from the "north" to produce some evidence of this from somewhere else. They will not find any in the Egyptian records.

NOTES ON CHAPTER FIVE

[Unless otherwise stated, all the plates referred to in the notes for this chapter are from the Oriental Institute, University of Chicago: *Medinet Habu*, 1930-1970.]

The following abbreviated references are used in this chapter:

Hood   S. Hood, *The Minoans* (1971).

Schachermeyr F. Schachermeyr, "Hörnerhelme und Federkronen als Bedeckungen bei den 'Seevölkern' der ägyptischen Reliefs," *Ugaritica VI* (1969).

Yadin   Y. Yadin, *The Art of Warfare in Biblical Lands* (New York, 1963).

1. W.F. Albright, "Dunand's New Byblos Volume: A Lycian at the Byblian Court," *BASOR*, 155 (1959): 31ff.

2. G.A. Wainwright, "Some Sea Peoples and Others in the Hittite Archives," *JEA*, XXV (1939): 148ff.

3. R.D. Barnett, "The Sea Peoples," *Cambridge Ancient History*, vol. II, chapter XXVIII; Schachermeyr, pp. 451ff.

4. Plate 44.

5. Plates 32-34.

6. Yadin, pp. 339f.

7. W. Helck, *Die Beziehungen Ägyptens zu Vorderasien im 3. und 2. Jahrtausend v. Chr.* (Wiesbaden, 1971²), pp. 230f.

8. Plate 37.

9. B. Landström, *Ships of the Pharaohs* (1970), pp. 111f; H.H. Nelson, "The Naval Battle Pictured at Medinet Habu," *JNES*, 2: 40ff.

10. Plate 11.

11. Plate 17.

12. Plate 35.

13. Plate 31.

14. Plates 32-34.

15. Schachermeyr, pp. 453f. G.A. Wainwright had drawn attention to this and other details of their dress in *JEA* 47 (1961).

16. W. Wreszinski, *Atlas zur altägyptischen Kulturgeschichte*, Teil II, (1935), Tafel 83 and 84, detail on Tafel 87.

17. R. Giveon, *Les Bédouins Shosou des documents égyptiens* (1971), pp. 54f.

18. E. Meyer, *Bericht über eine Expedition nach Ägypten* (1913), *Darstellungen der Fremdvölker*, photograph 191.

19. J. Pritchard, ed., *The Ancient Near East in Pictures* (1954), fig. 326 and p. 289.

20. Plate 18.

21. Hood, fig. 68.

22. Hood, plate 91; also Yadin, p. 344.

23. H. Frankfort, *The Art and Architecture of the Ancient Orient*, (1954), pp. 152f; C. Decamps de Mertzenfeld, *Inventaire commenté des ivoires phéniciens* (1954), plate LXIX.

24. Yadin, pp. 344f; T. Dothan, "Egyptian and Philistine Burial Customs," in *Proceedings of the Third International Colloquium on Aegean Prehistory*, "The 'Sea Peoples' and Events at the End of the Aegean Bronze Age," publication forthcoming.

25. T. Dothan, *The Philistines and Their Material Culture* (1967) and M. Dothan, "Ashdod. A City of the Philistine Pentapolis," *Archaeology*, 20 (1967).

26. E.D. Oren, *The Northern Cemetery of Beth-Shan* (1973).

27. J. Lagarce, "Note sur les rapports entre Chypre et les Philistins: quelques céramiques d'Enkomi et d'ailleurs" in *Proceedings of the Third International Colloquium on Aegean Prehistory*, "The 'Sea Peoples' and Events at the End of the Aegean Bronze Age," publication forthcoming.

28. J.D. Muhly, "The Philistines and Their Pottery," in *Proceedings of*

the Third International Colloquium on Aegean Prehistory, "The 'Sea Peoples' and Events at the End of the Aegean Bronze Age," publication forthcoming.

29. Schachermeyr, note 3.

30. R. Grosjean, "Recent Work in Corsica," *Antiquity* 40 (1966): 190ff.

31. M. Makkay, "The Distribution of the Horned Helmet in the Late Bronze Age of the Carpathian Basin" in *Proceedings of the Third International Colloquium on Aegean Prehistory,* "The 'Sea Peoples' and Events at the End of the Aegean Bronze Age," publication forthcoming.

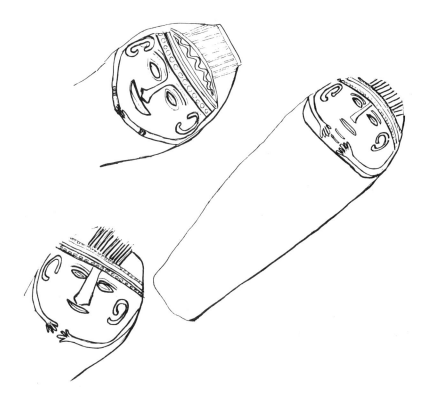

Figure 20. Anthropoid sarcophagi from Palestine showing the same markings as the feathered headdresses of the warriors in the Egyptian reliefs. It is interesting to note that the Philistine pottery has never been found together with these sarcophagi.

Egyptian Shipping

We have so far referred to Egyptian shipping only in the briefest terms by saying that the so-called Sea Battle from the time of Ramesses III, shown on the walls of the Medinet Habu temple, took place, according to the texts, *inside* the Great Green, in the streams of the Nile and not on the high seas. This is what the Egyptian texts themselves tell us, a fact completely overlooked by many historians so far. We have also said that the Egyptian monuments often associate Asiatics with boats.

Yet the whole way of life in Egypt was dependent on boats, of all shapes and sizes and to suit every activity associated with a man's everyday life. All transport of men and animals and food and building materials was by water. Military expeditions usually travelled on the river. The Pharaoh made his appearances on the royal barge. And every man's last journey was by water.

The ancient Egyptians' complete dependence on boats led to unlawful borrowing at times, as we know from the penalties laid down for people who unlawfully requisitioned boats: among other punishments, their noses could be cut off for this offence.[1]

Egyptian boats had to be as varied in type as the multiplicity of a man's needs demanded, and we find many names in the Egyptian texts for the different kinds of boats that were used on the river. However, they have not yet been studied in their contexts so we really do not understand their exact meaning, nor do we know the names of their parts nor the names of the individual constituents of the crew.

124

There is no reason to think that Egypt's obvious expertise on the Nile automatically extended to the sea. We pointed out earlier, in our chapter on the Delta, that Egypt was an inland country which stopped where the Nile stopped, before its waters became lost in the swamps of the Delta.

All our ideas that the Egyptians sailed on any sea must be set aside. They are not founded on what the texts tell us, but on assumptions related to a loose acceptance of the texts. Contrary to what has often been upheld, there is absolutely no evidence for sea-going by the ancient Egyptians at any time in their history from the pharaonic period.

It has been suggested that the Egyptians had access to the Red Sea by carrying or trailing their boats and provisions through the Wadi Hammamat, all 160-odd waterless kilometres of it![2] To say nothing of their journey back from that dry and desolate coast. We know that quarrying expeditions went half-way into this valley for a distance of about 80 kilometres, a point at which the greater part of all the inscriptions from this area are to be found.[3] But we can understand the need for an effort to obtain building stone even in difficult conditions. No such need is obvious in attributing to the Egyptians access to the Red Sea. Nor is there the slightest evidence for it. It is not enough to postulate Punt, as someone will surely do at this point. We do not know where Punt was situated, and we are still only theorizing about its whereabouts and talking about possibilities. Consequently this speculation cannot serve as a basis for any conclusions on shipping. What we must do is to look at the facts and the texts.

To begin with, the Palermo Stone tells us that forty ships laden with timber were received in Egypt,[4] not that Egyptian ships were sent to get it. There is total silence in the records about pharaonic sea-faring activity at all times.

We have already stated in our chapter on the Great Green that the Egyptians did not even have a word for 'sea' until they adopted the Semitic word ym after the Hyksos period in Egypt.

But what is surely most significant is the fact, that, together with the absence of a word for 'sea', we should also have the absence of any god to protect sea-farers, at any period in Egypt's history. This fact alone should have made scholars think again before suggesting that the ancient Egyptians went to sea. Only once does an Egyptian text speak of a deity of the sea, and it is of the Asiatic goddess Astarte that it speaks.[5] It is a unique text and even in this story, intended for Egyptian ears, the sea is portrayed as a greedy monster, insatiable of tribute which it keeps swallowing up. This picture of the sea is one which might be expected among an inland people.

No one would deny that Egypt imported timber, cattle, metals and other products from the earliest dynastic times and perhaps even before that. The records and the objects suggest this. But nowhere do the records mention any Egyptian ship on the sea.

The second Kamose Stela tells us that when the last Hyksos ruler Apophis was being driven out of Avaris, which Dr. Habachi has argued persuasively was on the site of the present Khata'na-Qantir, in the eastern Delta, the Egyptian fleet of Kamose was sent to plunder the pehu-land of Avaris. Kamose tells us:

> I did not leave a single plank belonging to the hundreds of ships [the text says 300 ships] of new cedar, filled with gold, lapis-lazuli, silver, turquoise and innumerable bronze battle-axes apart from moringa-oil, incense, fat, honey, itrn-wood, śśndm-wood, spny-wood, and all the precious wood of theirs, and all the good products of Retenu.[6]

At this time therefore we find hundreds of Asiatic ships coming to Egypt with their products.

Yet even in the time of Wenamun there is not a single reference to an Egyptian ship on any sea. Any time that a ship is referred to, it is an Asiatic ship with an Asiatic crew. Wenamun's ship had an Asiatic captain and very probably an Asiatic crew as well.

It is some years now since Dr. Faulkner's article appeared,[7] in which he discussed for the first time many details concerning boats and water transport in Egypt.

In recent years we have had the painstaking analysis of the structure of boats of all periods in ancient Egypt by Dr. B. Landström, who, surprisingly, does not make a crucial issue of the fact that the Egyptian boat had no keel.[8] We owe his study largely to the encouragement he received from Professor T. Säve-Söderbergh, himself the author of a book on the Egyptian navy of the eighteenth dynasty.[9] This is one of the few books we have on Egyptian water transport. The pioneering work in this field was done by C. Boreux in the early twenties,[10] following upon G. A. Reisner's catalogue of model ships and boats which had appeared ten years earlier.[11]

Strabo was among the earliest writers to comment on the coastline of the Delta along the Mediterranean Sea.[12] He summarised the position with regard to Syrian ships wishing to enter the Delta from the sea by telling us that the coast was low-lying with reefs and shallows and without harbours. In Strabo's time it was generally believed that the Egyptians excluded foreigners "like all barbarians." Strabo wisely thought that this absence of harbours along the coast contributed very much to the perseverance of this belief.

Only the great harbour of Alexandria was deep and close to the shore so that a large ship could be moored at the steps, once it was managed to sail through the very narrow passage which subsequently became a fortified site. At the time of the Napoleonic survey the port of Alexandria had already suffered damage as a result of earthquakes and subsidence, the consequences of which enlarged the strait and filled the interior of the basin with débris and let the sea in.[13] At the present time, the port lies well under water and the submerged remains of the Pharos have been studied by Miss Honor Frost and are shortly to be published.

It is quite startling to read in the Napoleonic survey of this area that the Alexandrian port of Eunoste could not be entered with the same wind that brought a ship down from Syria. But Asiatic shipping must have been able to enter the Delta at some point and it is logical to think that they would have sought the eastern Delta rather than the port of Alexandria. A glance at our map (fig. 4) will show that this is a reasonable assumption.

There may well have been, in earlier times, a way into the Delta through the Tanitic or Pelusiac mouths (or perhaps through both) which would have suited the direction of a favourable wind from Syria. Another arm of the Nile has recently been traced by two Israeli geologists, a defunct branch of the Pelusiac arm, crossing the deltaic plain east of the Suez canal at about 26 kilometres south of Port Said and extending from the El Baqar Canal to Tell el Farama (ancient Pelusium).[14] Ancient ruins in the area were found to be closely associated with the courses. This also may have been a point of entry at some stage in Egypt's history.

There is no evidence that any ships used along the western Asiatic coast were manned by any but Asiatic crews, probably of mixed provenance. This was true certainly up to the time of Wenamun.

The axe-head studied by A. Rowe, "of the boat-crew of Cheops or Sahure,"[15] cannot be taken as evidence of sea-going Egyptian crews. It is a single example of its kind, found near the Roman bridge at the mouth of the river Adonis. It cannot represent more than a "souvenir" of Egypt brought back by an Asiatic envoy, or an object lost by some exceptional Egyptian traveller, not necessarily of the same period as the object itself. We know that tomb robbery was rife during the Ramesside period, for example, from the account of the trial that has come down to us.[16] We also know that it was common for a Nile boat-crew to have a name and to be referred to by the particular gang they belonged to.[17] It is therefore more likely that the axe-head comes from a Nile boat-crew, for which we have similar evidence, than from a sea-going ship, for which we have none.

Wenamun sets out on his journey to the Lebanese coast on a ship whose captain's name is Mengebet, not an Egyptian name,[18] even though the ship was setting out on the Pharaoh's business. The prince of Byblos asks Wenamun where his cedar ship and its *Syrian* crew were, suggesting clearly that Syrian crews were normal at the time on ships coming from Egypt. When Wenamun insists that none but Egyptian crews sail under the orders of the Egyptian official Ne-su-Ba-neb-Ded, we can sense that he is prevaricating. He is protesting too much. This is confirmed by the retort from the prince of Byblos who silences him with:

> Aren't there twenty ships here in my harbour which are in commercial relations with Ne-su-Ba-neb-Ded?. . . . As to this Sidon, the other (place) which you have passed, aren't there fifty ships there which are in commercial relations with Werket-El and which are drawn up to his house?[19]

It is interesting to note that there are, at this troubled time, no less than 70 Levantine ships plying a trade with Egypt. The same story tells us that seven complete tree trunks constituted a full load for a ship travelling to Egypt. This must have been the normal load because some Assyrian reliefs show a fleet of small ships each carrying seven tree trunks, each with a hole pierced through one end (see fig. 15).[20] Four were loaded overhead, serving as a kind of hogging-truss, while three were towed in the water behind the ship. This appears to have been the normal practice, confirming that these ships would have been no bigger than a lorry and smaller than some of the Nile boats and royal barges mentioned in the records.

The late Professor John Barns stressed in his inaugural lecture at Oxford[21] that the Egyptians had a very real fear of dying abroad, because they would thereby miss the necessary burial rites to ensure their life in the hereafter. For example, the essential opening of the mouth ceremony was traditionally carried out by the dead man's heir. Only he could be relied upon to perform such an important rite.

The Mortuary Temple Edict of Amenophis III contains the worst curse he could think of on any violators of his endowment: "They shall be engulfed in the Great Green. They shall not receive the mortuary ceremonies of the righteous."[22] Death by drowning seems to have precluded such rights, as the body was lost. Even during the period of the Aton heresy, the burial rite was important. We find in the tomb of Mai: "May his lord give him burial, (for) his mouth was full of truth."[23]

Each of the very few texts we have referring to Egyptians abroad reflect this fear of dying away from Egypt. The Serpent has to comfort the Shipwrecked Sailor by telling him that he would die in his native town. The Pharaoh sends a messenger to Sinuhe to tell him to return to Egypt so that he may die in his native land.[24] From the sixth dynasty, we have the text in which Pepinakht tells us that the Pharaoh had sent him into Asiatic territory to bring back the body of the Egyptian official whom these foreigners had killed. The Kings of Egypt persistently refuse to allow any Egyptian princesses to go north to marry even the most powerful rulers of the northern countries, as we see from the Amarna Letters. They themselves were willing to marry Asiatic princesses, so it was not Pharaonic pride which influenced them. It is the fear of death abroad, without the proper burial rites, which decides for them, although this is never stated explicitly in the reasons they give.

But it is the story of Wenamun, late though it is, that is most revealing in this respect.[25] It is clear that the Near Eastern states are well acquainted with this Egyptian attitude to death. The prince of Byblos reminds Wenamun that he might die in the middle of the sea (lines 15-20), knowing well that the Egyptian thought this was the worst thing that could happen to him. Even the prince's butler taunts Wenamun about the terrors of the sea (lines 50-55). The prince asks his butler to show their visitor the tomb of the messengers of Kha-em-Waset, who were detained for seventeen years away from Egypt and died in Byblos. Such a thought is so painful to Wenamun that he cannot bring himself to look at it.

It is significant that even as late as this period the hero refers to the Mediterranean as "the great ym of Kharu," this sea being firmly linked with Syria in his mind and in the mind of the Egyptians for whom he is telling his story. Only in his official capacity as representative of the Pharaoh does Wenamun argue with the prince of Byblos by saying that the ym belongs to Amon, and even then, it is quite clear that he means it only in the same loose sense in which he claims that the Lebanon belongs to Amon.

The earlier, fifth dynasty documents from the Sahure reliefs have often been offered as evidence of sea-going by the ancient Egyptians.[26] Unfortunately only fragments remain of scenes which would have been of the greatest interest to us. The largest of the boat fragments shows four vessels of moderate size carrying some Egyptian sailors, some Asiatics (including women and children) and some Egyptian interpreters.[27] We would all agree that the pictorial evidence from the Egyptian reliefs and paintings cannot always be taken literally. Yet experience is teaching us more and more that the Egyptians paid a great deal of attention to detail as a general rule. The Asiatics shown on this group of four ships like the Egyptians are freely paying homage to Sahure as we can see from the position of their hands (fig. 2). These Asiatics are clearly not prisoners. Since the inscriptions over these boats take the trouble to label quite a number of Egyptians as imy-r ʿw, or interpreters, it is most likely that these Asiatics were in Egypt with their families as skilled men to work or advise, as we know they did from early times in the Sinai and elsewhere.

It is usually assumed that these Asiatics had just arrived in Egypt, Borchardt having originally suggested that this scene showed the return of an Egyptian fleet from abroad.[28] However, it is far more likely to be an Asiatic gang being moved from one place of work to another. It is otherwise inconceivable that foreigners just arriving in Egypt should not be exhibiting their gifts for the Pharaoh, who must, judging from their attitudes, have been standing right in front of them. Gifts were mandatory for visiting foreigners and for messengers from other countries.[29] None of the boats in the Sahure reliefs are carrying any foreign or exotic goods, no jars, nothing to show that they had made any contact with a foreign country. Nor do any of these vessels show any provisions stored on deck, as was usual, for a possible journey out. There are some fragments from this tomb showing Syrian jars and mountain bears, but unfortunately they are not in any defined context, and drawn on a much larger scale than the boats. They are undoubtedly gifts from Asiatic countries which could have been brought at any time. Sahure is called "Smiter-of-Foreign-Countries" in an inscription from the Sinai (Maghara), but this need mean no more than that his troops had defeated or driven out the Asiatics from some part of Lower Egypt. Asiatic prisoners, bound in the usual way, also appear elsewhere in this tomb.

All the boats in the Sahure reliefs show the bipod mast to be in the horizontal resting position, including, naturally, the ones in which the sailors are rowing and which Borchardt describes as "ausfahrende Schiffe."[30] This absence of sails would certainly indicate that the vessels were going downstream, but this does not mean that they were necessarily going to the open sea. They could have been going to a harbour somewhere in the Delta or perhaps a junction of waterways from which it was possible to set out for the Sinai along the same route as that followed by the Shipwrecked Sailor, who began his journey along the Great Green, which, we have to insist, must have been some part of the Delta. There must have been a harbour somewhere near Saft el Hennah and it is to be hoped that in the course of time we may learn more about these areas. As we have already said earlier, we must not exclude the possibility that the Egyptians travelled eastwards by water along the Wadi Tumilat during the period of the Old Kingdom. We may recall in this context the sixth dynasty inscription in which Uni tells us that he moved his troops in boats to get them to the north of the rebel Asiatic Beduin, in order to attack them successfully.[31]

The use of the hogging-truss on many Egyptian boats has usually been mistakenly understood to be a sign that they were sea-going ships. The hogging-truss was understood to be a means of strengthening the Egyptian boat against the waves of the sea, because it had no keel.

However, we must begin by stressing that the hogging-truss

is essentially a river device. The traditional papyriform Egyptian boat was such that it could be pulled well out of the water on to the muddy bank of the river without too much of its bottom getting stuck in the mud. This advantage, however, was offset by the danger of hogging when the boat was carrying a heavy load or the current was flowing rapidly while the boat was still moored by means of a peg driven into the mud, still today the normal way of mooring even a large boat along the Nile. The hogging-truss was also vital when the boat had to be dragged over a mud slipway to avoid a cataract or difficult river conditions, as Vercoutter found at Mirgissa, where we can still see a slipway five kilometres long.[32] Hogging-trusses are shown in the reliefs on quite small boats, as Dr. Landström himself illustrates from the tomb of Nefer in Saqqara and also Zaweit el Meitin.[33]

However, the example which conclusively illustrates how the Egyptians used the hogging-truss is the record of Hatshepsut's boat carrying the obelisks, which is shown to have a considerable number of hogging-trusses side by side, to carry the enormous weight.[34] This boat or boat complex has been estimated as weighing together 372 tons. The unit is recorded as having been 120 cubits long (63 metres) and 40 cubits wide (21 metres). These reliefs are unfortunately very fragmentary, but enough is left to show beyond any doubt the many hogging-trusses used on that occasion, which we know took place on the Nile and not on the sea.

It is usually suggested that Tuthmosis III travelled by ship on the Mediterranean on his northern campaigns because in the report of his sixth campaign the word "expedition" has the determinative of a boat.[35] We must remember that most expeditions took place along the Nile and this was the normal way of writing it. In the same way, the determinative of the pair of legs was used for any movement, including the flow of water or the flight of a bird. The reported visits in the annals of Tuthmosis III to Syrian harbour towns are not to be taken as proof of sea travel on his part, but as a routine pattern of his activity. The reports themselves follow a rigid order. The recording of the Pharaoh's visits to the harbours always follows the list of tribute from the Retenu and seems to suggest that he personally liked to supervise or show his presence at the time when these goods were loaded on the ships which were to take them south. Nowhere is it suggested that he travelled on the ships. These passages are to be seen in the context of the whole report of the campaign, and not as isolated paragraphs, unrelated to the rest.

On these tribute lists of goods for despatch to Egypt Asiatic ships of three types are mentioned: Keftiu-ships, Byblos ships and Sektu-ships.[36] Säve-Söderbergh does not favour the idea that the ships carrying these goods were Syrian and prefers to interpret the text in the sense that these ships were of Egyptian origin, purely on the grounds that there is little evidence of Syrian shipping at this time, in spite of the existence of the Byblos ship. However, there is abundant evidence for Asiatic shipping and bustling piratical activity along the coast by rival cities only one hundred years later in the Amarna letters, but still none at all for Egyptian sea-faring.

Säve-Söderbergh tries to make a case for Egyptian sea-faring during the Amarna period with a passage from Letter 288, by suggesting an amendment[37] in which it would seem that the Egyptians were a power to contend with at that time. However, although it seems he is right in his proposed amendment of this text, the total result does not make the best sense. It is possible to make better sense of this text, if the first line quoted by this scholar is taken with the preceding line of this letter with the result:

> . . . the enemy is pressing down upon me because (when) there is a ship in the middle of the sea. The strong hand of the King used to seize Nahrin and Kapasi. But now the Hapiru seize the cities of the King.

The general content of the Amarna Letters is that when Abdi-Ashirta's sons set up a blockade along the Western Asiatic coast, the ships of the cities still loyal to the Pharaoh left and took refuge in Egypt.[38] The letters are full of complaints about the seizure of ships of one state by another, and full of requests to the Pharaoh to send archers and men. It is significant that only one or two of the letters ask the Pharaoh to "send ships"[39] and that there is not a single reference to the presence of an Egyptian ship in those waters. Again we have total silence regarding Egyptian ships on the sea. Moreover, Aziru, one of Abdi-Ashirta's sons and a leader of rebel groups in this area, offers to the Pharaoh provisions in the form of ships, oil, boxwood and other woods,[40] which must, by implication, have been items very acceptable to the Egyptian ruler, and not otherwise available to him.

There can be no doubt that there was considerable ship-building activity in Egypt at most times. S. R. K. Glanville published a British Museum Papyrus (BM 10056)[41] which records details of a large boat-building centre in the Delta during the eighteenth dynasty. The records include the building or repairing of Byblos, Keftiu and Sektu ships, which no one would deny were sea-going ships. In this papyrus the text keeps referring to the lake on which the ships were being repaired or built and it is clear that some of the timber was being re-used.

This centre records the worship of Baal and Astarte among the gods, signifying a considerable number of Asiatics among the workmen.[42] One of the chief workmen here was from Arzawa (Irtw) while another main official was called Shebybaal, meaning "Baal has returned." Glanville suggested that this might be a reference to the return of the Asiatics to an area which may have been previously an Asiatic centre. Shebybaal appears to have worked directly under the orders of the officer in charge who was called Amenophis. Glanville reasonably argues from the evidence that this may well have been the son of Tuthmosis III.[43]

This boat-building centre also possessed a large store, called p3 mstyr.[44] The use of this word, among other things, led Glanville to conclude that this papyrus about ship-building came from the same chancellery as the papyrus Petrograd 1116 A and B. Apart from the interesting point made that the term p3 mstyr was to be found in these papyri only and in no others, Glanville remarked that in Petrograd 1116 B Vo the storehouse is said to be carrying supplies of ivory and ebony as well as decorative wood for ships. The British Museum papyrus mentions Syrian woods such as mr and ꜥš. It is therefore possible that this store may have been a receiving depot for all kinds of goods from the Asiatic countries.[45]

Not so convincing is Glanville's argument that the dockyard itself was called prw nfr.[46] Glanville tended to the view that the port had given its name to the town. The text shows it to have been more likely that prw nfr was the name of a boat. Nevertheless it is beyond dispute that a town called prw nfr did exist in the Delta. W. Spiegelberg, in his short but effective study, brought forward many texts to prove this.[47] Also this scholar warned us that although the records showed that the gods worshipped at this boat-building centre were those of the New Kingdom, there was no reason to assume that the town dated from that time and no earlier.

There are other references to ship-building in the Egyptian texts. From the sixth dynasty an inscription tells us that an Egyptian official was supervising the building of a Byblos ship "in the land of the Asiatics"[48] which, as we have already said in an earlier chapter, may well have been that part of Retenu extending into Lower Egypt, the t3 mḥw of the Nine Bows. If this is so, then such a site in the eastern Delta could have been the same site as that mentioned in the record from the time of Tuthmosis III, later on.

In a Middle Kingdom text, Henu has to get to the Great Green before he can make or reach his boat. We would say that this too could be referring to the same general area.[49]

The Papyrus Harris, dating from around the time of the death of Ramesses III, contains two references to ship-building, both similar to each other, but one more interesting than the other because it refers to the building of ships *inside* the Great Green, which we believe is again significant.[50]

In his original setting out of this problem in his book on the Egyptian navy of the eighteenth dynasty, Säve-Söderbergh discusses the possible geographical location for this boat-building centre.[51]

It is reasonable to suppose that ship-building would take place on navigable water or not too far from it, and in sheltered conditions. It is also reasonable to think that such a centre with its store of imported goods would be a reception area for foreign ships carrying foreign cargoes and especially timber. It is improbable that this could have been very far inland.

Also we must not rule out a strong Asiatic interest in such a centre and port. Dr. Aharoni gives a graphic picture of the Palestinian coast with its absence of harbours and natural anchorages.[52] He describes this shoreline as almost straight, with no bays, with a high ridge often rising sharply behind a narrow beach. At other times, there may be shifting sands for a depth of several miles inland, which would also prevent an approach to the shore. We might almost say that only Ashkelon, Joppa, Dor and Acco were suitable for use as ports by the local people. This makes it all the more likely that Asiatic tribes or cities without access to such harbours found other ways into Egypt, by land, perhaps, as far as the Bitter Lakes, and then by boat along the

Wadi Tumilat, during the times when this was in use.

Before concluding our remarks on shipping we must refer briefly to another very significant fact, namely, that no anchors have ever been found in any pharaonic Egyptian context, either in a natural or in a sacred setting, as have been found in Byblos, Ugarit, Cyprus and elsewhere.[53] I have related Miss Frost's work on Bronze Age anchors to the Egyptian setting elsewhere,[54] and we cannot do otherwise than conclude that very few Egyptians must ever have gone abroad to Byblos or to any other Asiatic countries. If they did go, it was only as dutiful servants of the Pharaoh, carefully counting the days and the hours before their return home.

NOTES ON CHAPTER SIX

The following abbreviated references are used in this chapter:

Borchardt	L. Borchardt, *Das Grabdenkmal des Königs Sahure* (Leipzig, 1913).
Breasted	J. Breasted, *Ancient Records of Egypt* (Chicago, 1906).
Gardiner	A.H. Gardiner, *Late Egyptian Stories* (Brussels, 1932).
Glanville I	S.R.K. Glanville, "Records of a Royal Dockyard of the Time of Tuthmosis III, Papyrus B M 10056," *ZAS* 66 (1930).
Glanville II	S.R.K. Glanville, "Records of a Royal Dockyard of the Time of Tuthmosis III," Papyrus B M 10056, *ZAS* 68 (1932).
Goyon	G. Goyon, *Nouvelles inscriptions rupestres du Wadi Hammamat* (Paris, 1957).
Knudtzon and Mercer	J.A. Knudtzon, *Die El Amarna Tafeln* (Leipzig, 1908) and S.A.B. Mercer, *The Tell el-Amarna Tablets* (Toronto, 1939).
Landström	B. Landström, *Ships of the Pharaohs* (London, 1970).
Rowe	A. Rowe, *A Catalogue of Egyptian Scarabs* (Cairo, 1936).
Säve-Söderbergh	T. Säve-Söderbergh, *The Navy of the Eighteenth Egyptian Dynasty* (Uppsala, 1946).
Sethe	K. Sethe, *Urkunden der 18. Dynastie*, (Leipzig, 1906-).
Wilson	J.A. Wilson (trans.), J.B. Pritchard, ed., *Ancient Near Eastern Texts Relating to the Old Testament* (Princeton, 1969³).

1. H. Kees, *Ancient Egypt* (London, 1961), pp. 103f, 194.
2. Goyon, pp. 1f.

3. Goyon, pp. 6f.

4. H. Schäfer, *Ein Bruchstück altägyptischer Annalen* (Berlin, 1902), p. 30.

5. Wilson, pp. 17f; Gardiner, pp. 76ff.

6. L. Habachi, *The Second Stela of Kamose* (Glückstadt, 1972), pp. 37f.

7. R.O. Faulkner, "Egyptian Sea-going Ships," *JEA*, 26 (1940): 3ff; also R.D. Barnett, "Early Shipping in the Near East," *Antiquity*, XXXII (1958): 128ff, who warns against this view.

8. See Landström. This book has an excellent bibliography on this subject.

9. See Säve-Söderbergh.

10. C. Boreux, *Études de nautique égyptienne* (Cairo, 1924-5).

11. G.A. Reisner, *Models of Ships and Boats* (Cairo, 1913).

12. Strabo 17.I.3.

13. *Description de l'Egypte,* ed. Panckoucke (Paris, 1829), vol. V, p. 209.

14. A. Sneh and T. Weissbrod, "Geological Survey of Israel," in *Science,* 180:59 (1973); also short report in the *Times* (London) 24 May 1973.

15. A. Rowe, *A Catalogue of Egyptian Scarabs* (Cairo, 1936), pp. 283 f.

16. T.E. Peet, *The Great Tomb Robberies of the Twentieth Egyptian Dynasty* (Oxford, 1930).

17. Rowe, pp. 284f.

18. J. Leclant, "Relations entre l'Egypte et la Phénicie," *The Role of the Phoenicians in the Interaction of Mediterranean Civilizations,* ed. W.A. Ward (Beirut, 1968), pp. 9ff.

19. Wilson, pp. 27f.

20. A. Salonen, *Die Wasserfahrzeuge in Babylonien* (Helsingfors, 1939), plates XVIIIff.

21. J.W.B. Barns, *Egyptians and Greeks,* 25 Nov. 1966.

22. From the limestone Stela BM No. 138, F. Chabas, *Mélanges Egyptologiques* (Chalon-sur-Saone, 1864), pp. 334f; also Breasted, vol. II, par. 925.

23. Breasted, vol. II, par 1003.

24. The story of *The Shipwrecked Sailor* and the story of *Sinuhe* may be found in recent translation by W. Kelly Simpson in *The Literature of Ancient Egypt* (Yale University Press, 1972).

25. Gardiner, pp. 61ff; Wilson, pp. 25ff.

26. See Borchardt.

27. Borchardt, Band 2, Blatt 11, 12.

28. Borchardt, Band 2, pp. 25f.

29. C. Zaccagnini, *Lo scambio dei doni nel Vicino Oriente durante i secoli XV-XIII* (Roma, 1973), pp. 45ff and 133ff.

30. Borchardt, Band 2, Blatt XI.

31. Sethe, *Urk I.* p. 104.

32. J. Vercoutter, *Mirgissa I* (Paris, 1970), pp. 173ff.

33. Landström, fig. 103 and R. Lepsius, *Denkmäler Ägypten und Äthiopien* (Leipzig, 1897-1913), vol. II, p. 108.

34. E. Naville, *The Temple of Deir El Bahari,* vol. VI (London, 1908), plates CLIII and CLIV; also Landström, pp. 128f.

35. Sethe, *Urk. IV,* p. 689.

36. Sethe, *Urk. IV,* p. 707.

37. Säve-Söderbergh, p. 40, from Amarna Letter 288.

38. J.A. Knudtzon, *Die El Amarna Tafeln* (Leipzig, 1908) and S.A.B. Mercer, *The Tell el-Amarna Tablets* (Toronto, 1939), Letters 101 and 155.

39. Knudtzon and Mercer, Letters 129 and 132.

40. Knudtzon and Mercer, Letter 160.

41. See Glanville I and II.

42. R. Stadelmann, *Syrisch-palästinesische Gottheiten in Ägypten* (Leiden, 1967), pp. 101f; also W. Helck, "Zum Auftreten fremder Götter in Ägypten," *Oriens Antiquus* V (1966): 1ff.

43. Glanville II, pp. 25f.

44. Glanville II, pp. 17f.

45. Glanville I, pp. 108f.

46. Glanville II, pp. 28f.

47. W. Spiegelberg, "La ville PRW-NFR dans le Delta," *Revue de l'Egypte Ancien,* 1 (1927): 215ff.

48. Sethe, *Urk, I,* p. 134; also *Göttinger Miszellen* 17 (1975): 39ff.

49. J. Couyat and P. Montet, *Les inscriptions hiéroglyphiques et hiératiques du Ouâdi Hammâmât,* Mém. Inst. Fr. 34 (1912), p. 83, line 14.

50. W. Erichsen, *Papyrus Harris I, Hieroglyphische Transkription,* Bibliotheca Aegyptiaca, V (Brussels, 1933), I:48, 6 and I:7, 8.

51. Säve-Söderbergh, pp. 37f.

52. Y. Aharoni, *The Land of the Bible* (London, 1967), pp. 9f.

53. H. Frost, "Bronze Age Stone-Anchors from the Eastern Mediterranean," *The Mariner's Mirror,* vol. 56, 4 (1970): 383f.

54. A. Nibbi, "Egyptian Anchors," *JEA,* 61 (1975).

Conclusion and Some Speculation

Who, then, were Egypt's attackers? Having seen from the texts that they were, beyond all doubt, western Asiatics called by Egypt the "northern hill-countries," we are still no wiser about their geographical homelands or the date of their settlement in the Delta. Nor do we really know much about their ethnic origins. *Asiatic* is a very vague term. We need help from scholars of western Asiatic archaeology and the Semitic languages.

A great deal has been written about the Lukka and the Philistines, assuming that they are the same people as the Peleset. One would like to see an objective study of these peoples from textual or other evidence that is *not* Egyptian. The material has been sparse, apart from references in the Egyptian texts. But we have now a growing body of archaeological material, and some texts, which, studied separately from the Egyptian ones, ought to yield some useful results.

It is unfortunate that there is so much dependence on Egyptian dating. Sometimes, we feel, this is taken to be more firmly based than it really is.

In attempting identification from the Egyptian documents, we look back into the history of this country and find that a western Asiatic enemy was always there, as far as we have any records.

Something is surely to be learned from the "Execration" figurines and objects carrying the names of cities and states abhorrent to Egypt and smashed ritually at the appropriate time.

No one has yet done full justice to the work of Kurt Sethe for the Berlin Museum fragments[1] or of Georges Posener for those in Cairo and Brussels[2] and more recently, from Mirgissa,[3] which may be earlier than the others. These brief and fragmentary Middle Kingdom documents include many names of Asiatic cities and states as well as references to the Asiatics themselves. We find Ascalon mentioned[4] among the Berlin fragments while Tyre[5] and Akko[6] are to be found among the others. Since they all appear several times in the records of Egypt's troubles with her neighbours, it is difficult to see how these cities could possibly be absent from the concerted attacks of these groups on the occasions when these are listed by their specific names.

There are also a number of cities referred to in the Old Testament, like Zarethan,[7] which may have joined actively in the hostilities against the common enemy, Egypt, without having been mentioned previously in the documents of this country.

As far as the names themselves are concerned, we should remember that the rules for some of the sound changes in the ancient Semitic languages are still in the tentative stages of definition. Moreover we should like to stress once again the principle which applies to all languages. Some unexpected changes often take place when foreign names are adapted and vulgarized in a different language. These Semitic names certainly entered into popular and frequent use in Egypt during the Ramesside period.

Among the other peoples mentioned, it is the Ekwesh who have aroused most interest and discussion. Some scholars have accepted that the Ekwesh of the Egyptian monuments are the same people as the Ahhiyawa of the Hittite documents.[8] This is possible but we cannot yet be certain about it. Whether the Ahhiyawa and the Achaeans are the same people is another question again which we cannot discuss here. These problems will have to be solved absolutely independently of the Egyptian texts. These and other related linguistic problems are discussed in depth by the distinguished professors Crossland, Howink Ten Cate, Collinge and other scholars in the *Proceedings of the First International Colloquium on Aegean Prehistory* at Sheffield,[9] and debated further in a third similar Colloquium, also held at Sheffield.[10]

We have now reached a stage where scholars determined to keep the Sea Peoples, in disciplines other than Egyptology, should list their evidence for them. If they cannot compile such a list, for want of material, the Sea Peoples should be allowed to sink back into oblivion, where we believe they properly belong.

NOTES ON CONCLUSION AND SOME SPECULATION

The following abbreviated references are used in this chapter:

Posener I	G. Posener, *Princes et Pays d'Asie et de Nubie* (Brussels, 1940).
Posener II	G. Posener, "Les Textes de'Envoûtement de Mirgissa," *Syria* (1966).
Sethe	K. Sethe, *Die Ächtung feindlicher Fürsten, Völker und Dinge*, APAW (Berlin, 1926).

1. Sethe.

2. Posener I; for later discussion, see S.H. Horn, *The Relations between Egypt and Asia during the Egyptian Middle Kingdom*, Ph.D. thesis, Univ. of Chicago, 1951.

3. Posener II, pp. 277ff.

4. Ascalon, see Sethe, pp. 52, 53 and 57. This city was renowned for its large temple to Astarte, and it is possible that the name of the city comes from the Sumerian meaning "the place of the large temple." The earlier Bronze Age inhabitants of this city were Canaanites, therefore Semitic and circumcised. Later, we know, the city became one of the five Philistine city states. As well as being mentioned in the Execration Texts, it is mentioned in the Amarna Letters Nos. 287, 320-2, 370 and in a hostile context in Egyptian records from the time of Merenptah and Ramesses II. It is also mentioned on an ivory tablet in hieroglyphs, found at Megiddo (see G. Loud, *The Megiddo Ivories*, Chicago, 1939, No. 380). The records show that this city was a vigorous enemy at these times.

5. Tyre is another city famous for its temple, to Melqart. See Posener I, 82, E 35, where there is a reference to a prince of Ḏw3wj., This city too is mentioned in other documents from Egypt, as well as in the Amarna Letters 77, 89, 92, 114, 146, 147, 149 and 155. There can be no doubt of the importance and enterprise of this city during the Bronze Age, although the excavations are unfortunately difficult because the older levels are all submerged, making the work slow and difficult. It is mentioned on the Egyptian lists of enemies in the New Kingdom so that there can be no doubt of its vigorous hostility to Egypt when the opportunity presented itself.

6. Akko, see Posener I, 87, E 49 ref. a prince of ʿkj. This city had the largest and best natural harbour along this coast. That it was very important in the eyes of the Pharaoh is clear from the Amarna Letters. He sent help to save Akko from being taken from him by the hostile

coalition long before he sent any help to Byblos, which, we might expect, would be more important to him. The Bronze Age city lies north of the city of Acre of later times. Both Professors Dothan have begun excavations of the Bronze Age site and their published results should be of the utmost importance to our understanding of the near eastern states at this time.

7. Zarethan is mentioned in I Kings 4:12. It is referred to as a site near Adam in the account of the damming of the Jordan. Beth Shean, in Solomon's fifth district, is described as being "beside Zarethan beneath Jezreel." It is believed that the present-day Tell el Sai diyah may be that city. In the excavations by Dr. J.B. Pritchard, unfortunately interrupted because of the general situation, there were remains of a Canaanite city as well as of a later Israelite one. See *Expedition,* vol. 6, 2 (1964); also bibliography in *Encyclopaedia Judaica* (Jerusalem, 1971).

8. G.L. Huxley, *Achaeans and Hittites,* (Oxford, 1968²).

9. *Bronze Age Migrations in the Aegean, Archaeological and Linguistic Problems in Greek Pre-history,* ed. R.A. Crossland and Ann Birchall (London, 1973).

10. See *Proceedings of the Third International Colloquium on Aegean Prehistory,* "The 'Sea Peoples' and Events at the End of the Aegean Bronze Age," Sheffield, 1973, publication forthcoming.

ABBREVIATIONS

AAA	*Annals of Archaeology and Anthropology* (Liverpool, 1908-).
AASOR	*Annual of the American Schools of Oriental Research,* (New Haven, 1919-).
AfK	*Archiv für Keilschriftforschung* (Berlin, 1923-25).
AfO	*Archiv für Orientforschung* (Berlin, Vols IIIff., 1926-).
AJA	*American Journal of Archaeology* (Concord, N.H., etc., 1885-).
AJSL	*American Journal of Semitic Languages and Literature* (Chicago, 1884-1941).
Ann. Serv.	*Annales du Service des Antiquites de l'Egypte* (Cairo, 1899-).
AO	*Der alte Orient* (Leipzig, 1900-).
AOT	*Altorientalische Texte zum alten Testament,* 2nd ed., edited by H. Gressmann (Berlin and Leipzig, 1926).
APAW	*Abhandlungen der preussischen Akademie der Wissenschaften* (Berlin, 1804-).
AS	*Assyriological Studies,* Oriental Institute, University of Chicago (Chicago, 1931-).
BA	*The Biblical Archaeologist* (New Haven, 1938-).
BASOR (SS)	*Bulletin of the American Schools of Oriental Research* (1919-) *(Supplementary Studies* [1945]).
BIFAO	*Bulletin de l'institut français d'archéologie orientale* (Cairo, 1901-).
Bi. Or.	*Bibliotheca Orientalis* (Leiden, 1943-).
BMQ	*The British Museum Quarterly* (London, 1926-).
CAH	*The Cambridge Ancient History²,* (1960-).
Chr. d'Eg.	*Chronique d'Egypte* (Brussels, 1925).
GGA	*Göttingische gelehrte Anzeigen* (Göttingen, 1801-).
GM	*Göttinger Miszellen* (Göttingen, 1972-).
IEJ	*Israel Exploration Journal.* (Jerusalem, 1950-).
JA	*Journal asiatique* (Paris, 1822-).

JAOS	*Journal of the American Oriental Society* (New Haven, 1849-).
JARCE	*Journal of the American Research Center in Egypt* (Princeton, N.J., 1962-).
JBL	*Journal of Biblical Literature and Exegesis* (Middletown, Conn., etc., 1882-).
JCS	*Journal of Cuneiform Studies* (New Haven, 1947-).
JEA	*Journal of Egyptian Archaeology* (London, 1914-).
JEOL	*Jaarbericht, Vooraziatisch-Egyptisch Gezelschap "Ex Oriente Lux"* (Leiden, 1933-).
JESHO	*Journal of the Economic and Social History of the Orient* (Leiden, 1957-).
JNES	*Journal of Near Eastern Studies* (Chicago, 1942-).
JPOS	*Journal of the Palestine Oriental Society* (Jersalem, 1920-).
JQR	*Jewish Quarterly Review* (Philadelphia, 1952-).
JRAS	*Journal of the Royal Asiatic Society* (London, 1834-).
JSOR	*Journal of the Society of Oriental Reasearch* (Chicago, 1917-1932).
KUB	*Keilschrifturkunden aus Boghazköi*, I-XXXIV (Berlin, 1921-1944).
LSS	*Leipziger semitische Studien* (Leipzig, 1903-).
Luckenbill, *AR*	D.D. Luckenbill, *Ancient Records of Assyria and Babylonia* (Chicago, 1926-27).
MAOG	*Mitteilungen der altorientalischen Gesellschaft* (Leipzig, 1925-).
MDIAK	*Mitteilungen des deutschen Instituts für ägyptische Altertumskunde in Kairo* (Berlin, 1930-).
MDOG	*Mitteilungen der deutschen Orientgesellschaft,* (Berlin, 1898-).
MIO	*Mitteilungen des Instituts für Orientforschung* (Berlin, 1953-).
MM	*Mariner's Mirror* (London, 1911-).
MVAG	*Mitteilungen der vorderasiatischen-ägyptischen Gesellschaft* (Berlin, 1896-).
PEQ	*Palestine Exploration Quarterly* (London, 1869-).
PW	*Philologische Wochenschrift* (Leipzig, 1881-).
QDAP	*Quarterly of the Department of Antiquities in Palestine* (Jerusalem, 1932-).
RA	*Revue d'assyriologie et d'archéologie orientale* (Paris, 1884-).
RB	*Revue biblique* (Paris, 1892-).
RSO	*Rivista degli studi orientali* (Rome, 1907-).
RT	*Recueil de travaux relatifs à la philologie et à l'archéologie égyptiennes et assyriennes* (Paris, 1870-1923).
SBAW	*Sitzungsberichte der bayerischen Akademie der Wissenschaften* (Munich, 1871-).

SPAW	*Sitzungsberichte der preussischen Akademie der Wissenschaften* (Berlin, 1882-1938).
Untersuch.	*Untersuchungen zur Geschichte und Altertumskunde Aegyptens* (Leipzig, 1896-).
Urk.	*Urkunden des ägyptischen Altertums* (Leipzig, 1903-).
VT	*Vetus Testamentum* (London, 1951-).
WVDOG	*Wissenschaftliche Veröffentlichungen der deutschen Orient-Gesellschaft,* Berlin (Leipzig, 1900-).
WZKM	*Wiener Zeitschrift für die Kunde des Morgenlandes* (Vienna, 1887-).
ZAS	*Zeitschrift für ägyptische Sprache und Altertumskunde* (Leipzig, 1863-).
ZAW	*Zeitschrift für die alttestamentliche Wissenschaft* (Berlin, Giessen, 1881-).
ZDMG	*Zeitschrift der deutschen morgenländischen Gesellschaft* (Leipzig, 1847-).
ZDPV	*Zeitschrift des deutschen Palaestina-Vereins* (Leipzig, 1878-).

GENERAL BIBLIOGRAPHY

Abel, F.M. *Géographie de la Palestine*. Paris, 1933-1938.

Adam, S. "Recent Discoveries in the Eastern Delta." *Ann Serv* 55 (1958): 301-24.

———. "Report on the Excavations of the Department of Antiquities of Ezbet Rushdi." *Ann Serv* 56 (1959): 207-26.

Aharoni, Y. *The Land of the Bible: A Historical Geography*. London, 1967.

Albright, W.F. "An Anthropoid Clay Coffin from Saḥâb in Transjordan." *AJA* 36 (1932): 295-306.

———. "Dunand's New Byblos Volume: A Lycian at the Byblian Court." In *BASOR* 155 (1959): 31ff.

———. "Some Oriental Glosses on the Homeric Problem." *AJA* 54 (1950): 162ff.

———. *The Vocalization of the Egyptian Syllabic Orthography*. New Haven, 1934.

Aldred, C. "The Parentage of King Siptah." *JEA* 49 (1963): 41ff.

———. "Valley Tomb No. 56 at Thebes." *JEA* 49 (1963): 176ff.

Allibone, T.E. ed. *The Impact of the Natural Sciences on Archaeology*. London, 1970.

Alt, A. "Die Staatenbildung der Israeliten in Palästina." In *Reformationsprogramm der Universität Leipzig*. Reprinted in *Grundfragen der Geschichte des Volkes Israel*. Munich, 1970.

Amiran, R.B.K. "Tell el-Yahudiyeh Ware in Syria." *IEJ* 7 (1957): 93-97.

———. "The Pottery of the Middle Bronze Age I in Palestine." *IEJ* 10 (1960): 204-25.

——— et al. *The Ancient Pottery of Eretz Yisrael* (in Hebrew). Jerusalem, The Bialik Institute and the Israel Exploration Society, 1963.

——— and A. Eitan. "A Canaanite-Hyksos City at Tell Nagila." *Archaeology* 18 (1965): 113-23.

———. *Ancient Pottery of the Holy Land*. New Brunswick, 1970.

Asaro, F., Perlman, I., and Dothan, M. "An Introductory Study of Mycenaean IIIC 1 Ware from Tel Ashdod." *Archaeometry*, 13 (1971): 169-175.

Astour, M.C. *Hellenosemitica*. Leiden, 1965.

———. "New Evidence on the Last Days of Ugarit." *AJA* 69 (1965): 253ff.

Aström, P. "Relative and Absolute Chronology, Foreign Relations, Historical Conclusions." in *The Swedish Cyprus Expedition, IV/1D: The Late Bronze Age*. Lund, 1972, pp. 558-781.

———. "Comments on the Corpus of Mycenaean Pottery in Cyprus." *Acts of the International Archaeological Symposium, "The Mycenaeans in the Eastern Mediterranean."* Nicosia, 1973.

Bakir, Abd el-M. "Slavery in Pharaonic Egypt." Supplément aux *Ann Serv*, Cahier 18. Cairo, 1952.

Ball, J. *Egypt in the Classical Geographers*. Cairo, 1942.

Barnett, R.D. "Mopsos." *JHS* 73 (1953): 140ff.

————. "The Sea Peoples." in *CAH*, vol. II, chapter XXVIII, 1969.

Barns, J.W.B. *The Ashmolean Ostracon of Sinuhe*. London, 1952.

Beckerath, J. von. "Die Reihenfolge der letzten Könige der 19 Dynastie." *ZDMG* 106 (1956): 241ff.

————. "Queen Twosre as Guardian of Siptah." *JEA* 48 (1962): 70ff.

————. *Untersuchungen zur politischen Geschichte der zweiten Zwischenzeit in Ägypten*, Glückstadt, 1964.

————. "Tanis und Theben," *Ägyptologische Forschungen 16*, Glückstadt-Hamburg-New York, J.J. Augustin, 1951.

Bénédite, G. "Le couteau de Gebel el-'Arak." *Monuments Piot* 22, 1.

Benson, J.L. "A Problem in Orientalizing Cretan Birds: Mycenaean or Philistine Prototypes?" *JNES* 20 (1961): 73-84.

Biran, A. "Tel Dan." *IEJ* 22 (1972): 164-166.

———— and Negbi, O. "The Stratigraphical Sequence at Tel Sippor." *IEJ* 16 (1966).

Bisson de la Roque, et al. *Le trésor de Tod*. Documents et Fouilles, Institut français d'archéologie orientale, No XI. Cairo, 1953.

Bonfante, G. "Who Were the Philistines?" *AJA* 50 (1946).

Borchardt, L. *Das Grabdenkmal des Königs Sahure*. Leipzig, 1913.

Boreux, C. *Etudes de nautique égyptienne*. Cairo, 1924-25.

Bottero, J. "Les Inventaires de Qatna." *RA* 43 (1949): 1-40.

————. *Le Problème des Habiru*, 4e Rencontre Assyriologique Internationale, Paris, Cahiers de la Société Asiatique 12 (1954).

Brea, L.B. *Sicily before the Greeks*. London, 1957.

Breasted, J.H. Ancient Records of Egypt, 5 vols. Chicago, 1906.

British Museum. *A General Introductory Guide to the Egyptian Collection*. third ed. London, 1964.

British Museum. *Hieratic Papyri in the British Museum. Third Series., Chester Beatty Gift*. Ed. A.H. Gardiner. London, 1935.

Brunner, H., review of Z. Mayani, "Les Hyksos et le monde de la Bible." *AfO* 18 (1958): 434.

Buck, A. de. "The Judicial Papyrus of Turin." In *JEA* 23 (1927): 152ff.

Bull, R.J., "A Re-examination of the Shechem Temple," *BA*, 23 (1960): 110-19.

Calverley, A.M. and Broome, M.F. *The Temple of King Sethos I at Abydos*. 4 vols. (London and Chicago, 1933-58).

Caminos, R.A. *Late Egyptian Miscellanies*. (Oxford, 1954).

Carruba, O. "Wo lag Ahhiyawa?" In *Compte-rendu du XIème Rencontre Ass*. (Leiden, 1964).

Case, H & Payne, J.C., "Tomb 100; The Decorated Tomb at Hierakonpolis," *JEA* 48, 5.

Casson, L. *Ships and Seamanship in the Ancient World*. (Princeton, 1971).

Černý, J. *Ancient Egyptian Religion* (London, 1952).

———. "Egypt from the Death of Ramesses III to the End of the Twenty-first Dynasty," *CAH*, Chapter XXXV.

———. "Note on the supposed beginning of a Sothis period under Sethos I." In *JEA*, 47 (1961): 150ff.

———. *Ostraca hiératiques (Cat. gén. Mus. Cairo)*. Cairo, 1935.

———. "Papyrus Salt 124 (Brit. Mus. 10055)." In *JEA* 15 (2929): 243ff.

———. "Prices and Wages in Egypt in the Ramesside Period," *Journal of World History* (Paris, 1954).

———. "Semites in Egyptian Mining Expeditions to Sinai," *Archiv Orientalni*, 7 (1935): 384-89.

———. "La fin de la seconde dynastie ou la période sethienne," *Ann Serv*, 44 (1944): 293-98.

———. "The True Form of the Name of King Snofru," *RSO*, 38 (1963): 89-92.

Champollion, J.F., *Monuments de l'Egypte et de la Nubie*, I—IV (Paris 1835-45).

Chicago University, Oriental Institute. *Medinet Habu*. 4 vols. (Chicago, 1930-70).

———. *Reliefs and Inscriptions at Karnak*. 2 vols. (Chicago, 1936).

Couyat, J. and Montet, P. *Les inscriptions hiéroglyphiques et hiératiques du Ouâdi Hammâmât*, Mém. Inst. Fr. 34, 1912.

Crossland, R.A., "Immigrants from the North," in *CAH*, rev. ed. no. 60, Cambridge, 1967.

Dahood, M.J., "Ancient Semitic Deities in Syria and Palestine." in S. Moscati, ed., *Le antiche divinità semitiche*, Roma, 1958.

Davies, Norman de G., *The Tomb of Amenemhet* (London, 1915).

———. *The Tomb of Huy* (London, 1926).

———. *The Tombs of Two Officials* (London, 1923).

———. *Seven Private Tombs at Kurnah* (London, 1948).

———. *The Mastaba of Ptahhetep and Akhethetep at Saqqarah* (London, 1900).

———. *The Rock Tombs of Deir el Gebrawi*, I-II, London, 1902.

———. *The Rock Tombs of El Amarna V*, London, 1908.

———. *The Tomb of Ken-Amun at Thebes*, New York, 1930.

———. *The Tomb of Nakht at Thebes*, New York, 1917.

———. *The Tomb of Neferhotep at Thebes*, New York, 1933

———. *The Tomb of Rekh-Mi-Re at Thebes*, I-II, New York, 1943.

———. *Two Ramesside Tombs at Thebes*, New York, 1927.

Davies, N. de G. & Faulkner, R.O., "A Syrian Trading Venture to Egypt," *JEA* 33, 40.

Desborough, V.R. d'A. *The Greek Dark Ages*. London, 1972.

_____. *The Last Mycenaeans and their Successors*. Oxford, 1964.

Desborough, V.R. d'A. and Hammond, N.G.L., "The End of the Mycenaean Civilization and the Dark Age" *Cambridge Ancient History*, Rev. Ed. No. 13, Cambridge, 1962.

De Vaux, R. "La Phénicie et les Peuples de la Mer." *Mélanges de l'Université Saint-Joseph* (Beirut, 1969) T.XLV, fasc. 29, 1969, 481ff.

Dikaios, P. *Enkomi, Excavations 1948-1958*, vol. II: *Chronology, Summary and Conclusions*. Mainz am Rhein, 1971.

Dothan, M. "The Excavations at Nahariyeh, 1954-55," *IEJ*, 6 (1956), 14-25.

_____. "Some Aspects of Religious Life in Palestine during the Hyksos Rule," *Antiquity and Survival*, 2 (1957), 121-30.

_____. "Excavations at Azor, 1960," *IEJ* 11, 1961.

_____. "Quelques tombes de l'âge du fer ancien à Azor," *Bulletin de la Société d'Anthropologie* II, XIe série, 1961.

_____. *Ashdod II-III. The Second and Third Seasons of Excavations 1963, 1965. Soundings in 1967* (ʿAtiqot IX-X), Jerusalem, 1971.

Dothan, M. and Friedman, D.N. *Ashdod I. The First Season of Excavations*, (ʿAtiqot). Jerusalem, 1967.

Dothan, T. "Archaeological Reflections on the Philistine Problem." *Antiquity and Survival*, 2, 1957: 151-164.

_____. "Anthropoid Clay Coffins from a Late Bronze Age Cemetery near Deir el-Balah (Preliminary Report)." *IEJ*, 22 1972: 65-72.

_____. *The Philistines and their Material Culture*, Jerusalem, 1967 (In Hebrew with English Summary).

Dunand, M., *Fouilles de Byblos*, 2 parts, Paris, P. Guethner, 1939-58.

Edel, E. "Der geplante Besuch Ḫattušilis III in Äegypten," In *MDOG* 92 (1960): 15ff.

_____. "Die Stelen Amenophis II aus Karnak und Memphis mit dem Bericht über die asiatischen Feldzüge des Königs," *Zeitschrift des deutschen Palästina-Vereins*, Leipzig, 69, 1953.

Edel, E. and Maryhofer, M. 1971. "Notizien zu Fremdnamen in ägyptischen Quellen," *Orientalia*, 40: 1-10.

Edgerton, W.F. "Egyptian Phonetic Writing," *JAOS* 60, 1940.

_____. "The Government and the Governed in the Egyptian Empire," *JNES* 6, 1947.

_____. "The Strikes in Ramses III's Twenty-Ninth Year," *JNES* 10 (1951), 137ff.

Edgerton, W.F. and Wilson, J.A. *Historical Records of Ramesses III*. Chicago, 1936.

Eissfeldt, O. "Philister," *P.W.* 38 (1938), 2301 ff.

_____. "Philister und Phönizier," *AO* 34 (1936).

Erichsen, W. *Papyrus Harris I, Hieroglyphische Transkription Bibliotheca Äegyptiaca*, V, Brussels, 1933.

Erlenmeyer, M.-I. and H. "Über Philister und Kreter," *Orientalia* 29, 1960; 30, 1961; 33, 1964.

Erman, A. *Die Religion der Ägypter, ihr Werden und Vergehen in vier Jahrtausende*, Berlin and Leipzig, 1934.

———. *The Literature of the Ancient Egyptians*, tr. M. Blackman, London, 1927.

Faulkner, R.O., "Egyptian Seagoing Ships," *JEA* 26 (1940), 3.

———. "The Wars of Sethos I", *JEA* 33 (1947), 34ff.

Fischer, H.G., "Some Notes on the Easternmost Nomes of the Delta in the Old and Middle Kingdoms," *JNES*, 18 (1959), 129-42.

Fougerousse, J.L., "Etudes sur les constructions de Tanis," *Kêmi*, 5 (1935), 19-48.

Franken, F.J., *Palestine in the Time of the Nineteenth Dynasty*, (b) Archaeological Evidence (Cambridge Ancient History, Rev. Ed. No. 67), Cambridge 1968.

Franken, H.J. "The Stratigraphic Context of the Clay Tablets Found at Deir 'Alla," *PEQ* 22 (1964), 79ff.

Frankfort, H., "Egypt and Syria in the First Intermediate Period," *JEA* 12 (1926), 80-99.

———. *Cylinder Seals*, London, Macmillan, 1939.

———. *Art and Architecture of the Ancient Orient*, Baltimore, Penguin Books, 1955.

Frost, H., "Egyptian Anchors," *MM* 50, 242.

———. "From Rope to Chain — On the Development of Anchors in the Mediterranean," *MM* 49, 1.

Gardiner, A.H. *Admonitions of an Egyptian Sage*, Leipzig, 1909.

———. *Notes on the Story of Sinuhe*, Paris, H. Champion, 1916.

———. "The Defeat of the Hyksos by Kamose: The Carnarvon Tablet No. 1," *JEA* 3 (1916), 95-110.

———. and B. Gunn, "New Rendering of Egyptian Texts II, The Expulsion of the Hyksos," *JEA* 5 (1918), 36-56.

———. "The Supposed Egyptian Equivalent of the Name of Goshen," *JEA* 5 (1918), 218-23.

———. "The Delta Residence of the Ramessides," *JEA* 5 (1918), 127-38, 179-200, 242-71.

———. "The Geography of the Exodus: An Answer to Professor Naville and Others," *JEA*, 10 (1924), 87-98.

———. "Tanis and Pi-Ramesse: A Retraction," *JEA* 19 (1933), 122-28.

———. "The Astarte Papyrus," in *Griffith Studies*, pp. 74-85.

———. "Davies's Copy of the Great Speos Artemidos Inscription," *JEA* 32 (1946), 43-58.

———. *Ancient Egyptian Onomastica*, 3 vols. London, Oxford University Press, 1947.

———. *Egyptian Grammar*, 2nd ed. Oxford, University Press, 1950.

_____. T.E. Peet, and J. Černý, *The Inscriptions of Sinai*, 2 parts, London, Egypt Exploration Society, 1952-55.

_____. "The First Menthotpe of the Eleventh Dynasty," *MDIK* 14 (1956), 42-51.

_____. *The Royal Canon of Turin*, Oxford, 1959.

_____. *Egypt of the Pharaohs*, Oxford, Clarendon Press, 1961.

_____. "Once Again the Proto-Sinaitic Inscriptions," *JEA* 48, (1962), 45-48.

_____. *The Kadesh Inscriptions of Ramesses II*. Oxford, 1960.

_____. "Some Reflections on the Nauri Decree." In *JEA* 38 (1952), 24ff.

Garstang, J. and Gurney, O.R. *The Geography of the Hittite Empire*, London, 1959.

Gauthier, H., "Une tombe de la XIXe dynastie à Qantir (Delta)," *Ann Serv* 32 (1932): 115-28.

_____. "Les deux rois Kamose," in *Griffith Studies*, pp. 3-8.

Glanville, S.R.K., "Records of a Royal Dockyard of the Time of Tuthmosis III," *ZAS* 66 and 68.

Goedicke, H. "Was Magic used in the Harem Conspiracy against Ramesses III?" In *JEA* 49 (1963): 175ff.

_____. "Zur Chronologie der sogenannten 'Ersten Zwischenzeit'," *ZDMG* 112 (1963): 239-54.

_____. "The Alleged Military Campaign in Southern Palestine in the Reign of Pepi I (VI Dynasty)," *RSO* 38 (1963): 187-97.

Goetze, A. "Is Ugaritic a Canaanite Dialect?" *Language* 17 (1941): 134-37.

_____. *Kleinasien*, 2nd ed. München, C.H. Beck, 1957.

_____. "On the Chronology of the Second Millennium B.C.," *JCS* II (1957): 53-61, 63-73.

_____. "Remarks on Some Names in the Execration Texts," *BASOR* 151 (1958): 28-33.

_____. "Warfare in Asia Minor," *Iraq* 25 (1963): 124-30.

Gordon, C.H. "The Role of the Philistines," *Antiquity* 30 (1956): 22ff.

Goyon, G. *Nouvelles Inscriptions Rupestres du Wadi Hammamat*, Paris, 1957.

Greenberg, M. *The Hab/piru*, New Haven, American Oriental Society, 1955.

Griffith, F.Ll. "The Abydos Decree of Seti I at Nauri." In *JEA* 13 (1927): 193ff.

_____. *The Antiquities of Tell el-Yahudiyeh*, London, Egypt Exploration Fund, 1890.

_____. *Hieratic Papyri from Kahun and Gurob*, 2 vols. London, 1898.

Griffiths, J.G. *The Conflict of Horus and Seth*, Liverpool, 1960.

Grosjean, R. "Recent Work in Corsica." *Antiquity* 40 (1966): 190ff. and pls. xxix-xxxi.

Gurney, O.R., *The Hittites*, Baltimore, 1961.

Habachi L. "Khata'na-Qantir: Importance," *Ann Serv* 52 (1954): 443-559.

———. "Preliminary Report on Kamose Stela . . .," *Ann Serv* 53 (1956): 195-202.

———. "Two Graffiti at Sehel from the Reign of Queen Hatschepsut," *JNES* 16, 88.

Hall, H.R. "The Peoples of the Sea," in *Mélanges Champollion*, 297ff. Paris, 1922.

Hammad, M. "Découverte d'une stéle du roi Kamose," *Chr d'Ég*, 30 (1955): 108-208.

Hankey, V. "Mycenaean Pottery in the Middle East: Notes on Finds since 1951." *BSA* 62 (1967): 107f.

Hassan, S., "The Causeway of Wnis at Sakkara," *ZAS* 80, 136.

Hayes, W.C. *Glazed Tiles from the Palace of Ramesses II at Kantir*, Metropolitan Museum of Art, New York, Papers No. 3, 1937.

———. "Notes on the Government of Egypt in the Late Middle Kingdom," *JNES* 12 (1953): 31-39.

———. *The Scepter of Egypt*, 2 vols. New York, 1953-59.

———. *A Papyrus of the Late Middle Kingdom in the Brooklyn Museum (Papyrus Brooklyn 35.1446)*, Brooklyn, 1955.

———. "The Middle Kingdom," *CAH²* I, ch. 20.

———. "Egypt: From the Death of Ammenemes III to Seqenenre II," *CAH²* 2, ch. 2.

Hayes, W., M.B. Rowton, and F.H. Stubbings, "Chronology: Egypt; Western Asia; Aegean Bronze Age," *CAH²* I, ch. 6.

Helck, H.W. "Der Einfluss der Militärführer in der 18. ägyptischen Dynastie," *Untersuch*. 14, Leipzig, 1939.

———. *Zur Verwaltung des mittleren und neuen Reichs*, Leiden-Cologne, 1958.

Helck, W., *Die Beziehungen Ägyptens zu Vorderasien im 3. und 2. Jahrtausend v. Chr.*, Wiesbaden 1962.

———. "Die Sinai-Inschrift des Amenmose," *MIO* 2, 189.

———. "Zum Auftreten fremder Götter in Ägypten," *Oriens Antiquus V* (1966): 1.

Herzog, R. *Punt*, Glückstadt, 1968.

Hestrin, R. *The Philistines and other Sea Peoples*, Jerusalem, 1970.

Heurtley, W.A. "The Relationship between 'Philistine' and Mycenaean Pottery," *QDAP* 5 (1936): 90ff.

Hintze, F. "Die Felsenstele Sethos I bei Qasr Ibrim," in *ZAS* 87 (1962): 31ff.

Holland, L.B. "The Danaoi," *Harv. Stud. Clas. Phil.* (1928): 59ff.

Hölscher, W. *Libyer und Ägypter*, Glückstadt, 1937.

Holwerda, A.E.J. & Boeser, P.A.A., *Beschreibung der aegyptischen Sammlung des Niederländischen Reichsmuseums der Altertümer in Leiden, Atlas*, Leiden, 1926.

Hornell, J. "Egyptian Shipping of About 1500 B.C.," *MM* 23, 105.

_____. "Origins of Plank-built Boats," *Antiquity* 13, March, 1969.

_____. "The Frameless Boats of the Middle Nile," *MM* 25, 417, *MM* 26, 125.

_____. "The Making and Spreading of Dugout Canoes," *MM* 34, 46.

_____. *Water Transport*, Cambridge 1946.

Hornung, E. *Der Eine und die Vielen*, Darmstadt, 1971.

_____. *Untersuchungen zur Chronologie und Geschichte des neuen Reiches*, Wiesbaden, 1964.

Houwink ten Cate, Ph. H.J. *The Luwian Population Groups of Lycia and Cilicia Aspera during the Hellenistic Period (Documents et Monumenta Orientis Antiqui, 10)*, Leiden, 1961.

Hrouda, B. "Die Einwanderung der Philister in Palästina." In *Vorderasiatische Archäologie: Studien und Aufsätze: Festschrift Moortgat* (1965): 126ff.

Huxley, G.L. *Achaeans and Hittites*. Oxford, 1960.

James, F. *The Iron Age at Beth Shan. A Study of Levels VI-V*. Philadelphia, 1966.

James, T.G.H. *The Archaeology of Ancient Egypt*, London, 1972.

_____. "A Group of Inscribed Egyptian Tools," *BMQ* 24 (1961): 36-43.

_____. "Egypt: From the Expulsion of the Hyksos to Amenophis I," *CAH²*, 2, ch. 8.

Janssen, J.J. *Two Ancient Egyptian Ship's Logs*, Leiden, 1961.

Kantor, H.J. "The Aegean and the Orient in the Second Millennium B.C.," *AJA* 51 (1947): 1-103.

_____. "The Chronology of Egypt and its Correlation with that of Other Parts of the Near East in the Periods before the Late Bronze Age," in R.W. Ehrich, ed., *Relative Chronologies in Old World Archaeology*, Chicago, University of Chicago Press, 1953.

_____. "Syro-Palestinian Ivories," *JNES* 15 (1956): 153-74.

Karageorghis, V. "Horse Burials on the Island of Cyprus," *Archaeology*, 18 (1965): 282-90.

_____. "Recent Archaeological Investigations at Kition." In Κυπριακαί Σπουδαί (Nicosia, 1962).

Kees, H. "Tanis: Ein kritischer Überblick zur Geschichte der Stadt," *Nachr. Göttingen* (1944): 145-82.

_____. *Ancient Egypt, A Cultural Topography*, London, 1961.

_____. "Ein Handelsplatz des MR im Nordostdelta," *MDIAK* 18 (1962): 1-13.

_____. *Ägypten* (W. Otto, ed.) Handbuch der Altertumwissenschaft III,

Part 1, No. 3 Kulturgeschichte des alten Orients, I, Munich, 1933.

———. *Farbensymbolik in ägyptischen religiösen Texten*, Göttingen, 1943.

Kenyon, K.M. *Archaeology in the Holy Land*, London, 1965.

Kimmig, W. "Seevölkerbewegnung und Urnenfelderkultur," *Studien aus Alteuropa* (Cologne-Graz, 1964) 1, 220-83.

Kitchen, K.A. *Ramesside Inscriptions*, Oxford, 1968-

———. "Review of R. Herzog: Punt," *Orientalia*, N.S. 40, 1971.

———. "Some New Light on the Asiatic Wars of Ramesses II," *JEA* 50 (1964): 47ff.

———. "The Philistines." In Wiseman, D.J. (ed.), *Peoples of Old Testament Times* (London 1972).

———. *The Third Intermediate Period in Egypt (1100-650 B.C.)*. Warminster, 1973.

Knudtzon, J.A. *Die El-Amarna Tafeln*. Leipzig, 1915.

Koenig, J. "Aperçus nouveaux sur les Hyksos," *RA* 50 (1956): 191-99.

Lacau, P. "Une Stéle du roi 'Kamosis'," *Ann Serv* 39 (1939): 245-71.

Lambdin, T.O. review of Z. Mayani, *Les Hyksos et le monde de la Bible*, *JBL* 77 (1958): 272-74.

Landström, B. *Ships of the Pharaohs*, London, 1970.

Langdon, S. and Gardiner, A.H. "The Treaty of Alliance between Hattusili, King of the Hittites, and the Pharaoh Ramesses II of Egypt." In *JEA* 6 (1920): 170ff.

Leclant, J., and J. Yoyotte. "Les Obelisques de Tanis," *Kémi*, 14 (1957): 43-80.

Leibovitch, J. "Le Problème des Hyksos et celui de l'exode,"*IEJ* 3 (1953): 99-112.

———. "Deux nouvelles inscriptions protosinaïtiques," *Le Muséon* 74 (1961): 461-66.

———. "The Date of the Proto-Sinaitic Inscriptions," *Le Muséon* 76 (1963): 201-03.

Lepsius, R. *Denkmäler Ägypten und Äthiopien*, 5 vols. Leipzig, 1897-1913.

Loud, G. *Megiddo, II: Seasons of 1935-39*, 2 parts, Chicago, University of Chicago Press, 1948.

Lucas, A. *Ancient Egyptian Materials and Industries*, 4th ed., London, 1962.

Macalister, R.A.S. *The Philistines, their History and Civilisation* (with an introduction by Dr. Abraham Silverstein), Chicago, 1965.

Malamat, A. "Cushan Rishathaim and the Decline of the Near East around 1200 B.C.," *JNES* (1954) 231ff.

———. "The Period of the Judges." in Mazar, B. (ed.), *The World History of the Jewish People* III: *Judges* (New Brunswick 1971): 129-163.

———. "Western Asia Minor in the Time of the Sea Peoples." In *Yediet Bahaqirat Eretz: Israel Weatiqoteha*, 30 (1966): 195ff. (in Hebrew).

Maxwell-Hyslop, R. "Daggers and Swords in Western Asia," *Iraq*. 8 (1944): 1-65.

Mazar, B. "The Sanctuary of Arad and the Family of Hobab the Kenite." *JNES* 24 (1965): 297ff.

———. "The Philistines and the Rise of Israel and Tyre." In *The Israel Academy of Sciences and Humanities, Proceedings*, I, no. 7 (1964): 1ff.

———. "The Philistines and their Wars with Israel." In Mazar, B. (ed.), *The World History of the Jewish People* III: *Judges* (New Brunswick 1971): 164-179.

Mekhitarian, A. *Egyptian Painting*. Editions d'Art Albert Skira. Geneva, 1954.

Mitchell, T.C. "Philistia." In D. Winton Thomas (ed.), *Archaeology and Old Testament Study*. Oxford, 1967.

Montet, P. *Byblos et l'Egypte: quatre campagnes de fouilles à Gebeil, 1921-24*, 2 vols., Paris, 1928-29.

———. "Notes et documents pour servir à l'histoire des relations entre l'ancienne Egypte et la Syria," *Kêmi*, I (1928): 83-93.

———. "Tanis, Avaris et Pi-Ramses," *RB* 39 (1930): 1-28.

———. "La Stèle de l'an 400 retrouvée," *Kêmi*, 1 (1933): 191-215.

———. *Le Drame d'Avaris: Essai sur la pénétration des Sémites en Egypte*, Paris, 1941.

———. *Les Enigmes de Tanis*. Paris, 1952.

———. "Notes et documents, 'V. Byblos et le Keftioy," *Kêmi*, 13 (1954): 71-73.

———. "La Stèle du roi Kamose," *CRAIBL* (1956): 112-20.

———. *Géographie de l'Egypte ancienne*, 2 vols. Paris, 1957.

———. "Notes et documents, XI. Herichef a Byblos," *Kêmi*, 16 (1962): 89-90.

Moran, W.L. "Mari Notes on the Execration Texts," *Orientalia*, 26 (1957): 339-45.

Nelson, H.H. "The Naval Battle Pictured at Medinet Habu," *JNES* 2,40.

North, M. "Die syrisch-palästinische Bevölkerung des zweiten Jahrtausend v. Chr. im Lichte neuer Quellen," *ZDPV* 65 (1942): 0-67.

O'Callaghan, R.T. *Aram Naharaim: A Contribution to the History of Upper Mesopotamia in the Second Millennium* B.C., Rome, Pontificium Inst. Biblicum, 1948.

Oderwald, J. "Were the Egyptians Builders of Sea-going Ships?," *JEOL* 6, 35.

Oppenheim, A.L. "Sea-faring Merchants of Ur," *JAOS* 74 (1954).

Oren, E.D. "Tel Sera." *IEJ* 22 (1972): 167-69.

Ory, J. "Excavations at Ras el-Ain II," *QDAP* 6 (1938): 99-120.

———. "A Middle Bronze Age Tomb at El-Jisr," *QDAP* 12 (1946)

Otten, H. "Neue Quellen zum Ausklang des hethitischen Reiches," *MDOG* 94 (1963): 1ff.

Otto, H. "Die Keramik der mittleren Bronzezeit in Palästina," *ZDPV* 61 (1938): 147-277, Pls. 2-24.

Piggott, S. "The earliest wheeled vehicles and the Caucasian evidence," in *Proceedings of the Prehistoric Society* (Cambridge 1968) N.S. 34, 266-318.

Porter, B. and R.L.B. Moss, *Topigraphical Bibliography of Ancient Egyptian Hierogylphic Texts, Reliefs, and Paintings,* 7 vols., Oxford, 1927-51.

Posener, G. "Le canal du Nil à la Mer Rouge avant les Ptolomées," *Chron. d'Egypte,* 13, 1938.

———. *Princes et pays d'Asie et de Nubie,* Brussels, Fondation Egyptologique Reine Elisabeth, 1940.

———. *Littérature et politique dans l'Egypte de la XIIe dynastie,* Paris, Champion, 1956.

———. "Les asiatiques en Egypte sous les XIIe et XIIIe dynasties," *Syria* 34 (1957): 145-63.

———. "Nḥsyw et Mḏ3yw," *ZAS* 83 (1957): 38-43.

———. "Pour une localisation du pays Koush au Moyen Empire," *Kush* 6 (1958): 39-68.

———. J. Bottéro, and K.M. Kenyon, "Syria and Palestine c. 2160-1780 B.C.," *CAH*², 1, ch. 2f.

Pritchard, J.B. *Ancient Near Eastern Texts Relating to the Old Testament* Princeton, 3rd. ed. 1969.

———. "New evidence on the role of the Sea Peoples in Canaan at the beginning of the Iron Age." In: *The Role of the Phoenicians in the Interaction of Mediterranean Civilizations, Papers presented to the Archaeological Symposium at the American University of Beirut,* ed. W.A. Ward, Beirut, 1968, 99-112.

———. *The Ancient Near East in Pictures Relating to the Old Testament.* Princeton, 1954.

Quibell, J.E. *Archaic Objects,* I-II, Cairo, 1904-05.

———. *Excavations at Saqqara (1906-1907),* Cairo, 1908.

———. *Tomb of Yuaa and Thuiu,* Cairo, 1908.

Quibell, J.E. & Green, F.W., *Hierakonpolis II,* London, 1902.

Redford, D.B. *History and Chronology of the Eighteenth Dynasty of Egypt: Seven Studies.* Toronto, 1967.

———. "The Hyksos Invasion in History and Tradition," *Orientalia,* N.S. 39, 1970.

Reisner, G.A. *Models of Ships and Boats,* Cairo, 1913.

Riis, P.J. "L'activité de la Mission Archéologique Danoise sur la côte phénicienne." *Ann. Arch. de Syrie,* 8-9 (1954-59) and 10 (1960).

———. *Hama, III, 3. Les Cimetières à Crémation,* Copenhagen, 1948.

Rowe, A. *A Catalogue of Egyptian Scarabs in the Palestine Archaeological Museum*, Cairo, Impr. de l'Institut français d'archéologie orientale, 1936.

Rowton, M.B. "Comparative Chronology at the Time of Dynasty XIX," *JNES* 19 (1960): 15-22.

_____. "The Material from Western Asia and the Chronology of the Nineteenth Dynasty," *JNES* 25 (1966): 240ff.

_____. "The Background of the Treaty between Ramesses II of Egypt and Hattusilis III." *JCS* 13 (1959): 1ff.

Säve-Söderbergh, T. *Aegypten und Nubien*. Lund, 1941.

_____. *Egyptisk egenart*, Halmstad 1968.

_____. *Four Eighteenth Dynasty Tombs*, Oxford, 1957.

_____. *On Egyptian Representations of Hippopotamus Hunting as a Religious Motive*, Uppsala 1953.

_____. *The Navy of the Eighteenth Egyptian Dynasty*, Uppsala, 1946.

Schachermeyr, F. "Hörnerhelme und Federkronen als Kopfbedeckungen bei den 'Seevolkern' der Ägyptischen Reliefs." *Ugaritica* (Paris 1969) VI, 451-459.

Schaeffer, C.F.A. *Enkomi-Alasia* 1. Paris, 1952.

_____. "Götter der Nord und Inselvölker in Zypern." *AFO* 21 (1966): 59ff.

_____. *Ugaritica* V. Paris, 1949.

Schlott, A. *Die Ausmasse Ägyptens nach altägyptischen Texten*, Tübingen, 1969.

Schulman, A.R. "The Egyptian Chariotry: A Reexamination," *JARCE* 2 (1963): 75-98.

_____. *Military Rank, Title and Organization in the Egyptian New Kingdom*, Chicago, 1964.

Sethe, K. "Der Denkstein mit dem Datum des Jahres 400 der Ära von Tanis," *ZAS* 65 (1930): 85-89.

_____ *Die Ächtung feindlicher Fürsten, Völker, und Dinge auf atltägyptischen Tongefässcherben des mittleren Reiches*, Berlin Akad, Abhandlunger, 1926, No. 5.

_____. *Die altägyptischen Pyramidentexte*, Glückstadt, 1908-22.

Sethe, K. and Helck, W. *Urkunden der 18. Dynastie (Urk. IV)* Leipzig and Berlin, 1906-58.

Shafei, Aly Bey, "Historical Notes on the Pelusiac Branch," *Bulletin de la Société de Géographie d'Egypte*, 21 (1943-46): 231-85.

Simons, J. *Handbook for the Study of Egyptian Topographical Lists Relating to Western Asia*, Leiden, 1937.

Simpson, W.K. ed. *The Literature of Ancient Egypt*, New Haven, Yale Univ. Press, 1972

_____. "Reshep in Egypt," *Orientalia*, 29 (1960): 63-74.

_____. "Studies in the Twelfth Egyptian Dynasty: I. The Resistance of

Itj-towy," *JARCE* 2 (1963): 53-59.

Singer, C., and others, *A History of Technology,* Oxford, 1956.

Smith, W.S. *The Art and Architecture of Ancient Egypt,* Baltimore, 1958.

──────. "The Old Kingdom in Egypt," *CAH²,* 1, ch. 14.

──────. *Interconnections in the Ancient Near East: A Study of the Relationships between the Arts of Egypt, the Aegean, and Western Asia,* New Haven, Yale University Press, 1965.

Sommer, F. *Die Aḫḫijavā-Urkunden (Abh. München,* 1932.)

Staatliche Museen zu Berlin, *Führer durch das Berliner ägyptische Museum,* Berlin, 1961.

Stadelmann, R. *Syrisch-palästinensische Gottheiten in Ägypten.* Leiden, 1967.

Täckholm, V. *The Wood Reserves of Egypt in the Near East, Symposium sur la protection de la nature dans le Proche-Orient,* UNESCO; Beirut 1954.

────── and M. Drar, *Flora of Egypt, II,* Cairo, 1950.

Tadmor, H. "Philistia under Assyrian Rule," *BA* 29 (1966): 861.

Te Velde, H. *Seth, the God of Confusion,* Leiden, 1967.

Torr, C., *Ancient Ships,* Chicago 1964.

Tufnell, O. "Hyksos Scarabs from Canaan," *Anatolian Studies,* 6 (1956): 67-73.

──────. *Lachish IV: The Bronze Age,* Oxford, 1957.

──────. "The Courtyard Cemetery of Tell el-Ajjul, Palestine," *BIA* 3 (1962): 1-37.

Vandersleyen, C. *Les guerres d'Amosis,* Brussels, 1971.

Vandier, J. *Manuel d'archéologie égyptienne,* I-V, Paris, 1954-69.

Van Seters, J. *The Hyksos,* New Haven, 1966.

Vercoutter, J. *L'Egypte et le monde égéen préhéllenique.* Cairo, 1956.

──────. *Les Haou-nebout, BIFAO* XLVI and XLVIII, 1947 and 1949.

Vermeule, E. *Greece in the Bronze Age,* Chicago, 1964.

W. Vycichl, "Les emprunts aux langues sémitiques," *Textes et Langages de L'Egypte Pharaonique, Inst. Fr. Arch. Or.,* 1973.

──────. "L'origine du nom du Nil," *Aegyptus,* 1972.

Wainwright, G.A. "Caphtor, Cappadocia," In *VT* 6, a (1956): 200ff.

──────. "Caphtor, Keftiu and Cappadocia." In *PEFQS* (1931): 203ff.

──────. "Keftiu." In *JEA* 17 (1931): 26ff.

──────. "Keftiu and Karamania (Asia Minor)," In *Anatolian Studies,* 4 (1954): 38ff.

──────. "Keftiu: Crete or Cilicia?" In *JHS* 57 (1931): 1ff.

──────. "The Keftiu People of the Egyptian Monuments." In *Ann. Arch. Anthr.* 6 (1913): 24ff.

──────. "The Teresh, the Etruscans and Asia Minor," *Anatolian Studies,* 9, 1959.

_____. "A Teucrian at Salamis in Cyprus," *JHS* 83, 1963.

_____. "The Coming of Iron," *Antiquity*, March, 1936.

_____. "Some Sea-Peoples and Others in the Hittite Archives," *JEA* XXV, 1939.

_____. "Merneptah's Aid to the Hittites," *JEA* 46 (1960): 24ff.

_____. "The Meshwesh," *JEA* 48 (1962): 89ff.

_____. "Shekelesh or Shasu?" *JEA* 50 (1964): 40ff.

_____. "Some Sea-Peoples." *JEA* 47 (1961): 71ff.

_____. "Some Early Philistine History," *Vetus Testamentum* 9, 1959.

Waldbaum, J. "Philistine Tombs at Tell Fara." In *AJA* 70 (1966): 331ff.

Ward, W.A. "Comparative Studies in Egyptian and Ugaritic," *JNES* 20 (1961): 31-40.

_____. "Egypt and the East Mediterranean in the Early Second Millennium B.C.," *Orientalia*, 30 (1961): 22-45, 120-55.

_____. "Egypt and the East Mediterranean from Predynastic Times to the End of the Old Kingdom," *JESHO* 6 (1963): 1-57.

_____. "Review of Helck's *'Die Beziehungen Äegyptens'*," *Orientalia* 33 (1964): 135-40.

Wolf, W. *Die Bewaffnung des altägyptischen Heeres*, Leipzig, 1926.

Wreszinski, W. *Atlas zur altägyptischen Kulturgeschichte*, Part II, Leipzig, 1935.

Wright, G.E. "Philistine Coffins and Mercenaries." In *Bi. Or.* 22 (1959).

_____. (ed.) "The Archaeology of Palestine." In *The Bible and the Ancient Near East: Festschrift, W.F. Albright* (New York, 1961): 85-139.

_____. "Fresh Evidence for the Philistine Story," Biblical Archaeologist 29, 1966.

Yadin, Y., "Hyksos Fortifications and the Battering-Ram," *BASOR* 137 (1955): 23-32.

_____. "Excavations at Hazor, 1955-58," *IEJ* 6 (1956): 120-25; ibid., 7 (1957): 118-23; ibid. 8 (1958): 1-14; ibid. 9 (1959): 74-81.

_____. *The Art of Warfare in Biblical Lands in the Light of Archaeological Study*, New York, McGraw-Hill, 1963.

_____. *Hazor*, 4 vols. Jerusalem, Hebrew University, 1958-63.

Yoyotte, J. "A propos du panthéon de Sinouhé," *Kêmi* 17, 1964.

_____. "Les Stèles de Ramsès II à Tanis," *Kêmi* X, 1949.

_____. "Une epithète de Min comme explorateur des régions orientales," *Revue d'Egyptologie*, IX, 1952.

INDEX